MONTH-BY-MONTH
READING
AND WRITING
FOR KINDERGARTEN
SYSTEMATIC, MULTILEVEL INSTRUCTION

by

Dorothy P. Hall

and

Patricia M. Cunningham

Project Coordinator
Joyce Kohfeldt
I.E.S.S., Kernersville, NC

Editor
Tracy Soles

Senior Editor
Chris McIntyre

Illustrators
Melinda Fabian
Pam Thayer

DEDICATION

This book is dedicated to kindergarten teachers everywhere and especially those teachers who have shared ideas with us and whose superb teaching inspired the writing of this book. There are many whose names we have forgotten—or, in some cases, never knew. But we learned from the questions they posed and the solutions they offered.

Particular thanks goes to Elaine Williams, kindergarten teacher extraordinaire! Thanks Elaine, this book would never have happened without you!

Thanks also to Michelle Hall, beginning kindergarten teacher and daughter extraordinaire!

Special thanks to the following teachers with whom we have worked most closely during the past ten years:

Audrey Anderson	Catherine Davis	Elizabeth Rieker
Lynn Boyles	Dawn Eichelberger	Johnetta Sinclair
Ann-Parke Busby	Kim Fansler	Mary Ware
	Carolyn Henderson	
	Susan Poholsky	

ISBN 0-88724-398-3

TABLE OF CONTENTS

INTRODUCTION

It's the first day of kindergarten! For some parents, it is the day when they will have to separate from their child and watch him or her begin a long journey towards literacy. For other parents whose children have been attending a "learning center" or "preschool" since birth, it is now time for the first day of "real" kindergarten or "real" school. Whatever the preparation, it is a big day for both parents and youngsters! The children, as little as they are, know that this is a big day for them. Some are nervous and scared; but almost all are excited to begin this journey.

The teachers are excited, too, and most are still apprehensive, even after years of teaching kindergarten. What will the parents expect from kindergarten? What do these eager little bodies want from their first "real" teacher? Everyone knows that what happens in kindergarten will make a big difference for these students!

The reading and writing activities in this book will help all students begin or continue on their literacy journey. The activities described are **multilevel** activities. A multilevel activity is one where there are **multiple things to be learned** and **multiple ways for children, no matter what their current stage of development, to move forward.**

These activities are also developmentally appropriate, meaning the curriculum is carefully framed on knowledge of children's physical, social, and intellectual growth. It is based on what children need to learn and what is known about how children learn.

A developmentally appropriate kindergarten is like a good home, where children can learn through playing, cooking, watching, listening, acting, reading or pretend reading, and writing or pretend writing. It is a place where they can explore their environment, ask questions, and answer questions. It is a place where the teacher is like a parent: reading to the children and talking about the stories they read; writing for the children and allowing them to write for different purposes; having time to explore the community on field trips, and talking about those experiences together. It is a place where children clean up after themselves, learn more about familiar and unfamiliar topics (usually called themes), and learn more about what interests them most—themselves. Most importantly, it is a place where children learn that reading provides both enjoyment and information, and they develop the desire to learn to read and write.

Learning to read and write appears effortless for some children. For other children, it is a struggle. Recent findings from emergent literacy research have demonstrated that children who learn to read easily have had a variety of experiences with reading and writing before coming to school which enable them to profit from school literacy instruction ("Emergent Literacy" by Elizabeth Sulzby and W. M. Teale, *Handbook of Reading Research, Vol. II*, 1991). From these experiences, children develop critical understandings which are the building blocks of their success.

Unfortunately, not all children have had home experiences through which they can develop these understandings. In developmentally appropriate kindergartens, teachers provide a variety of experiences which simulate as closely as possible those at-home reading and writing experiences so that all children develop critical understandings.

> The goal of a developmentally appropriate kindergarten is to accept all children where they are and take them forward on their literacy journey.

Throughout the book, you will see how phonics and spelling develop through early reading and writing activities. Using these multilevel activities, you will be able to meet the needs of all children in your kindergarten class, regardless of their ability level.

Hopefully, each month you will find the time to read daily *to* your children, to read *with* your children using predictable big books, and provide opportunities for your children to read or "pretend read" *by themselves*.

So that all children make progress in writing, it is suggested that **you model "how to write" by writing a morning message at the beginning of the day and/or a journal entry at the end of the day. Besides writing <u>for</u> children, you can also write <u>with</u> children when they do shared writing and make predictable charts. Once these writing activities occur, children are ready to write by themselves, so you need to provide opportunities for them to do so.**

Emergent readers learn about letters, sounds, and words when they read nursery rhymes and rhyming books and talk about rhyming words. Focus on letter names and letter sounds as you talk about the names of the children in the class and the familiar words you encounter during the opening and shared reading with predictable books. By asking, "What do you notice?" when talking about letters, words, and sentences, you encourage all children to contribute, regardless of their ability level. Finally, as you work with environmental print (cereals, restaurants, and names), you give all children an opportunity to practice letters and "reading" even if they come from a home without books.

The first day of kindergarten is here—THE BIGGEST DAY FOR THE LITTLEST CHILDREN IN ELEMENTARY SCHOOL!! Teachers scurry to get all the pieces in place and the room decorated. Are the bulletin boards up? Are the centers in the right place? Books, beads, puzzles, and boxes need to be within reach. Meanwhile, parents scurry to get haircuts, physicals, school supplies, and new outfits for their kindergarten kids as they head off to school. HERE COME THE KIDS!

Kindergarten children at all different literacy levels must sense that they are making progress if their eagerness and excitement is to sustain them through the hard work of learning to read and write.

In this chapter, we will describe activities for the first 4-6 weeks of school that help develop critical concepts and strategies, while simultaneously convincing ALL children that they can successfully learn about reading and writing in kindergarten. Kindergarten teachers have successfully used these activities with children at all stages of development.

THE OPENING

The kindergarten day begins in different ways in different classrooms. Some teachers start the day in centers, others choose to open with "big group." **To follow the activities in this book, it is recommended that you call the children together at the front of the room and begin the day as one big, happy group.**

- **"Who is here today?"**
- **"Is anyone absent?"**
- **"What day of the week is it?"**
- **"What is the month? the date? the year?"**
- **"How many days have we been in school? Can anyone count them? Let's make a mark (or tally mark) for each day."**

Some teachers mark the days by adding straws to a jar—one straw per day. They allow the children to bundle the straws in groups of ten with a rubber band, as the days progress, so that children learn to count by ones and tens and later bundle the tens together to form a hundreds group. In this way, children learn about ones, tens, and hundreds for "real reasons." Have your calendar near the big group so that the students can look at it and talk about the days of the week and the date and chart the weather for the day (sunny, cloudy, windy, rainy, snowy, cold, cool, warm, or hot, etc.). Talk with your students about any plans and special events for the day. Discuss what book will be read aloud, what the students will do in centers, or what the students will learn about the current theme.

How The Opening Is a Multilevel Activity

During the opening, kindergarten children learn about the reading and writing of both numbers and words. What each child learns depends upon what each child already knows. While some children are learning numbers and number words, others are learning something about the letters and sounds at the beginning of these words. Still other students are learning to read or spell the words that are discussed and written on the chalkboard, or written on word cards and put in a pocket chart. The same is true for the days of the week, the months, the weather, and the current theme. In kindergarten, learning about reading and writing is done in an integrated way; and you can teach this during the opening.

READING ALOUD TO CHILDREN

Children love books and stories. Kindergarten teachers have always recognized the importance of reading a variety of books to their students. **Reading to children promotes oral language and concept development, adds to the student's store of information about the world, and helps students develop a sense of story.** Research tells us that children who come to schools ready to read come from homes where they have been read to (*Beginning To Read: Thinking and Learning About Print* by Marilyn Jager Adams, MIT Press, 1991).

Your local or school library is filled with many children's books, some of which have been favorites of children for years. These are the books you need to share with your students. For example, as a kindergarten child, you probably loved to listen to the teacher read *Curious George* books. Children enjoy watching how George's curiosity gets him into trouble. They also learn the meaning of the word *curious*.

Children need both good stories (fiction) and informational books (nonfiction). Some children really like stories, while other children like to learn more about their world. Books can take children as far away as the Yangtze River in *The Story About Ping* by Marjorie Flack and Kurt Weise (Viking Press, 1961) or Africa in *A is for Africa* by Ifeoma Onyefulu (Cobblehill Books, 1993), or as near as the local zoo or farm.

Just as parents sit close to their children while reading to them, so should teachers. Sitting close to the teacher and the book helps children to focus. If children are not used to having books read to them, you may have to talk to them about being good listeners. Kindergartners need to be told that you have lots of students, so there are different rules at school than there are at home. The students will need to listen first, then ask their questions. **Children at all levels can learn from listening to, talking about, and thinking about all different kinds of books.**

Favorite Books for August/September:

Country Fair by Gail Gibbons (Little, 1994).

Curious George by H.A. Ray (Houghton Mifflin, 1973).

Franklin Goes to School by Paulette Bourgeois (Scholastic, Inc., 1995).

Hungry Caterpillar, The by Eric Carle (Scholastic, Inc., 1987).

I Started School Today by Karen G. Frandsen (Children's Press, 1984).

Kindergarten Kids by Ellen Sensi (Scholastic, Inc., 1994).

Little Engine That Could, The by Watty Piper (Putnam Publishing Group, 1984).

Miss Nelson Is Missing by Harry Allard (Scholastic, Inc., 1977).

Monster Goes to School by Virginia Mueller (Albert Whitman, 1991).

My Brown Bear Barney by Dorothy Butler (Greenwillow Books, 1989).

Real Mother Goose, The (Rand McNally & Company, 1916, 1944, 1976).

School Bus by Donald Crews (Greenwillow Books, 1984).

School Days by B. G. Hennessy (Viking Press, 1990).

This Is the Way We Go to School by Edith Baer (Scholastic, Inc., 1990).

Timothy Goes to School by Rosemary Wells (Dial Books, 1981).

Wheels on the Bus, The by Raffi (Crown, 1990).

Where the Wild Things Are by Maurice Sendak (Scholastic, Inc., 1963).

READING WITH CHILDREN—Shared Reading with Predictable Big Books

Children who were read to before beginning school were usually sitting on someone's lap or snuggled up next to someone. Being read to in this way allowed them to look at pictures and print up close. They asked questions and talked about the book, often relating the book to their own lives. They asked for the same book to be read over and over again, many times, until they could almost read the book by heart. They knew if the reader skipped a paragraph or page of their favorite book. They would then stop the reader to say, "You forgot . . ." and immediately turn back to the page so that the reader could "read it right." The parents of these children can often remember their child's favorite book even several years later. For example, as a three-year-old, Michelle's favorite book was *In A People House* by Dr. Seuss (Random House, 1989). Michelle is now a kindergarten teacher, and her parents can still recite the words from the book by heart!

One particular kind of reading especially important for kindergartners is **shared reading with predictable big books. Predictable books are books with repeated patterns, refrains, pictures, and rhymes. Shared reading of predictable big books is an extension of the "lap experience" children had at home.** The children can see both the pictures and the print as the teacher reads the book. And, just like at home, one reading is never enough! After two or three readings, some kindergarten children naturally chime in, having memorized many of the words!

To illustrate the many types of activities you might do with a predictable big book, some examples with *Will You Be My Friend?* by popular children's author Eric Carle (Houghton Mifflin, 1991) are described in the following few sections. In the big book, a little gray mouse is looking for a friend. The mouse runs from animal to animal asking, "Do you want to be my friend?" Each animal has the same answer, "No." So, the mouse runs on. Finally, the mouse meets another little gray mouse who answers, "Yes"—just in time!

Choosing a big book for shared reading:

1. The book must be very predictable, with repetitive sentence patterns, pictures to support those sentence patterns, and not too much print.

2. The book should be enjoyable and appealing to most of the children in the class, since the entire class will work with the same big book.

3. The book must be able to "take students someplace" conceptually. Most teachers spend a week or two with a book—reading, rereading, acting out the story, and building connections to themes and units to extend the children's knowledge.

The most important goal for shared reading is that even children with no literacy background will be able to pretend read the book after it has been read to them several times and will develop the confidence that goes along with that accomplishment.

The repeated patterns, refrains, pictures, and rhymes in predictable books allow children to "pretend read" a book which has been read to them several times. **Pretend reading is a stage most children go through with a favorite book which has been read and reread to them by some patient adult.** Shared reading of predictable books allows all children to experience this pretend reading.

Read and Talk About the Book

As with any book, the first and second readings should be strictly focused on the meaning and enjoyment of the book. *Will You Be My Friend?* has delightful illustrations, and children enjoy the suspense of waiting to see if this poor little mouse will find a friend. It is also easy for the children to see how the big animals are not really suited to be the friend of a tiny mouse.

Encourage the Children to Join in the Reading

There are a variety of ways to encourage children to join in the reading. For this book, children will almost naturally want to say the repeated responses. After the first and second readings, the children will be chiming in every time the book says, "So the mouse ran on. Do you want to be my friend?" Encourage the students to do so! Remember, this is called shared reading!

As you are reading, do not call attention to what appears to be the green grass, as it is not grass but a snake which makes its move on the last page! Do talk about the different animals in the book. Some may be familiar to kindergarten children (horse, monkey) while others may not (hippopotamus, peacock). See if the children can predict the animal that will be pictured on the next page by the tail shown on the preceding page. Some children are better at this activity than others, but most enjoy doing it.

Act It Out

Young children are natural actors. They pretend and act out all kinds of things. Students do not need props or costumes to act out this particular story, but you may want to make some simple drawings on card stock or poster paper of the animals and the two mice. Laminate the cards, punch two holes at the top, and tie lengths of yarn through the holes. Children can hang the cards around their necks, and everyone will know what character they are! Act out the story several times, so that each student has a chance to be one of the animals or one of the mice. You should read the part of the book that is not repetitive and let children in the audience read the repetitive part with you, "So the mouse ran on. Do you want to be my friend?"

Make the Book Available

Make the big book, or little-book versions, available for children to read. Some teachers like to practice reading the story a few times with the class and then make a tape recording for the listening center in which the teacher reads the animals' answers and the whole class or small groups of children chime in for the repeated phrases. **Children delight in going to the listening center and listening to someone they know reading the book! Some children will just listen to the story, turning the page at the right time. Other children will be reading the words along with the voice(s) on the tape. Still other children may be matching the voices with the print on each page and really reading!**

How Shared Reading with a Predictable Big Book is Multilevel

During shared reading with a predictable big book, there are many different things to notice. Children who come to kindergarten already beginning to read move further along in their reading as they learn more words and begin to notice the similarities and differences in words. Children who come to kindergarten with little print experience learn what reading is and begin to develop their concepts of print. Others learn a few words and begin to notice how words are the same and different. Most importantly, **all children develop the desire to learn to read and the confidence that _they are learning to read_!**

Favorite Big Books for August/September:

Buttons, Buttons by Rozanne Lanczak Williams (Creative Teaching Press, 1994).

Five Little Monkeys Jumping on the Bed by Eileen Christelow (Clarion, 1989).

Gingerbread Boy retold by Brenda Parkes & Judith Smith (Rigby, 1984).

Goldilocks and the Three Bears retold by David McPhail (D. C. Heath, 1989, 1991).

I Can't Get My Turtle to Move! by Elizabeth Lee O'Donnell (Houghton Mifflin, 1991).

Little Red Hen by Janina Domanska (Houghton Mifflin, 1991).

Rosie's Walk by Pat Hutchins (Aladdin Paperbacks, 1968).

Sheep on a Ship by Nancy Shaw (Houghton Mifflin, 1989).

Three Pigs, The retold by Brenda Parkes and Judith Smith (Rigby, 1985).

Who's in the Shed? by Brenda Parkes (Rigby, 1987).

GETTING TO KNOW YOU!

Most kindergarten teachers begin the year with some get-acquainted activities. As part of these activities, teachers often focus on a special child each day. In addition to learning about each of their classmates, students can focus attention on the special child's name and use the name to develop some important understandings about words and letters.

To prepare for this activity, you should write all the children's first names (with initials for last names if two names are the same) with a permanent marker on sentence strips. Cut the strips so that long names have long strips and short names have short strips. Place the strips in a box. Each day, reach into the box and draw out a name. This child becomes the "Special Student for the Day" and his or her name becomes the focus of many activities. Reserve a bulletin board and add each child's name to the board as it is selected. Some teachers have children bring in a snapshot of themselves or take pictures of the children to add to the board as the names are added. Other teachers may have the class to make drawings of each "special child" so that they can put together a class book at the end of the activity. The teacher then titles this book "Our Class" and places it in the reading center for the students to enjoy.

Here are some examples of activities you might do with the students' names:

First Name/Day

Close your eyes. Reach into the box, shuffle the names around, and then draw one out. Call that child forward and name him or her "Special Student" for the day! Lead the other children in interviewing this child—find out what he or she likes to eat, play, do after school, etc. Does he or she have brothers? sisters? cats? dogs? mice? Now focus the children's attention on the special child's name—*Jasmine*. Point to the word *Jasmine* on the sentence strip and develop the children's understanding of jargon by pointing out that this **word** is Jasmine's name. Tell the students that it takes many **letters** to write the word *Jasmine* and let them help you count the letters. Say the letters *J-a-s-m-i-n-e* and have the children chant them with you. Point out that the word Jasmine **begins** with the letter **J**. Explain that the **J** looks bigger than the other letters because it is a **capital J** and the other letters are **small** letters (or **uppercase/lowercase** - whatever jargon you use).

Let Jasmine lead the class in a cheer with the letters in her name. "Give me a *J*." The children shout "J." "Give me an *a*." "Give me an *s*." "Give me an *m*." "Give me an *i*." "Give me an *n*," and finally, "Give me an *e*." "What have you got?" "Jasmine." "What have you got?" "Jasmine." "Yeh!"

Take a blank sentence strip and have the students watch as you write the word *Jasmine*. Have them chant the spelling of the letters with you. Cut the letters apart and mix them up. Let Jasmine arrange the letters in the right order so that they spell her name. Have the other children chant to check that the order is correct. Reshuffle the letters and let another student, perhaps someone Jasmine chooses, rearrange the letters in the correct order.

Give each child (including Jasmine) a large sheet of drawing paper, and let the students use crayons to write *Jasmine* in large letters on one side of the paper. Model at the board how to write each letter as they write it. Do not worry if what the children write is not perfect (or even bears little resemblance to what you wrote), and resist the temptation to correct what they write. Remember that children who write at home before coming to school often reverse letters and make them in funny ways.

> The important concept for students to understand is that names are words, that words can be written, and that it takes lots of letters to write words.

Finally, have everyone look at Jasmine and talk about what she is wearing. Then, let the children draw a picture of Jasmine on the other side of their drawing paper. Save the drawing Jasmine did of herself with her name printed on the back. Post Jasmine's name strip on the "Special Student" bulletin board, along with her drawing (and/or photograph). Let Jasmine take all the other drawings of her home!

Second Name/Day

Draw another name—*Ryan*. Whatever interviewing you did for Jasmine, do for Ryan. **(Decide carefully what you will do for the first child because every child will expect equal treatment!)**

Focus the students' attention on Ryan's name. Say the letters in *Ryan* and have the children chant them with you. Help the children to count the letters and decide which letter is first, last, etc. Let Ryan lead a cheer using the letters of his name. Write *Ryan* on another sentence strip and cut it into letters. Have Ryan arrange the letters to spell his name, then let him choose another child to do the same. The children can use the first sentence strip name (the one you drew from the box) as their model.

Put Ryan's name on the bulletin board under Jasmine's name and compare the two. Which name has the most letters? How many more letters are in the word *Jasmine* than in the word *Ryan*? Does *Ryan* have any of the same letters as *Jasmine*?

Finish the lesson by having everyone write *Ryan* on a sheet of paper. Have everyone look at Ryan and what he is wearing, then ask the students to draw Ryan's picture. Let Ryan take all the drawings home except for the drawing he did of himself, which will be posted on the bulletin board and may later become his page in the class book. (More information about class books on page 22)

Third Name/Day

Draw the third name—*Michelle*. Do the interviewing and chant the letters in Michelle's name. Let Michelle lead the class in a cheer using the letters of her name. Write her name again on a sentence strip, cut it up into letters, and do the letter arranging. Be sure to note the two *l*'s and two *e*'s and to talk about first and last letters. Which letter is the capital letter and where do you see, or find, the capital letter in Michelle's name?

As you put Michelle's name on the bulletin board, compare it to both Jasmine's name and Ryan's name. This is a perfect time to notice that all names begin with a capital letter but not always the same letter. If two names begin with the same letter, be sure to point out that not only do they begin with the same letter but they begin with the same sound! Finish the lesson by having the children write *Michelle* (copying your example on the board), and then draw Michelle's picture for her to take home, saving only Michelle's own drawing for the bulletin board and class book.

Fourth Name/Day

The name *David* is chosen next. Do all the usual activities. When you put David's name on the bulletin board, help the students to realize that Ryan still has the shortest name. (Ed may now look down at the name card on his desk and call out that his name is even shorter. You will point out that he is right, but that Ryan's name is the shortest one on the bulletin board right now.) **What is really fascinating about this activity is how the children compare their own names to the ones on the board even before their names are chosen. This is exactly the kind of word/ letter awareness you are trying to develop!**

Fifth Name/Day

Mike's name is drawn next. Do the various activities as you did before, and then take advantage of the fact that lots of words rhyme with *Mike*. Say pairs of words, some of which rhyme with Mike and some which do not rhyme: Mike/bike; Mike/hat; Mike/hike; Mike/boy; Mike/pike; Mike/Mary; and so forth. If the pairs of words rhyme, the students should point to Mike and shout, "Mike." If the words do not rhyme, the students should shake their heads and frown.

How Getting to Know You is Multilevel

"Getting to Know You" is truly a multilevel activity. All children learn the names of their classmates and also learn something about themselves on the day they are "spotlighted." Children learn to read and write many of the names, and as they focus on which names have which letter, they learn letter names, too. Students begin to associate letters and sounds with the names they are learning and to learn print concepts and jargon.

DEVELOPING PHONEMIC AWARENESS— Nursery Rhymes

The ability to recite nursery rhymes is considered an indicator of **phonemic awareness. Phonemic awareness develops through a series of stages during which children first become aware that language is made up of individual *words*, that words are made up of *syllables*, and that syllables are made up of *phonemes*.** It is important to note here that it is not the "jargon" children learn. Five year-olds cannot tell you there are three syllables in dinosaur and one syllable in bat. What they can do is clap out the three beats in dinosaur and the one beat in bat. Likewise, they cannot tell you that the first phoneme in bat is "b," but they can tell you what you would have if you took the *b* off bat—you would have *at*.

> One of the best indicators of how well children will learn to read is their ability to recite nursery rhymes when they walk into kindergarten!

Children develop this phonemic awareness as a result of the oral and written language to which they are exposed. Nursery rhymes, chants, and Dr. Seuss books usually play a large role in this development. **This month, read and share lots of nursery rhymes with your children.** Children should learn to recite the rhymes, sing the rhymes, clap to the rhymes, and pantomime the rhymes. In some kindergarten classrooms, they develop "raps" for the rhymes.

Once the children can recite lots of nursery rhymes, the nursery rhymes can then be used to teach the concept of **rhyme**. Divide the class into two halves—one half of the class says the nursery rhyme, but stops when they get to the rhyming word. The other half of the class waits to shout the rhyming word at the appropriate moment:

Jack and Jill

First Half: Jack and Jill went up the...

Second Half: hill.

First Half: To fetch a pail of water. Jack fell down and broke his ...

Second Half: crown.

First Half: and Jill came tumbling after.

Humpty Dumpty

First Half: Humpty Dumpty sat on a wall. Humpty Dumpty had a great...

Second Half: fall.

First Half: All the king's horses and all the king's men, Couldn't put Humpty together...

Second Half: again.

Children also enjoy making rhymes really silly by making up a new word that rhymes.

Jack be nimble. Jack be quick.
Jack jumped over Pat and Dick!

Nursery rhymes have been a part of our oral heritage for generations. **It is now known that the rhythm and rhyme inherent in nursery rhymes are important vehicles for the beginning development of phonemic awareness. Nursery rhymes should play a large role in any kindergarten curriculum.**

How Nursery Rhymes are Multilevel

Nursery rhymes are as multilevel as what the teacher does with them. First, chant the nursery rhymes with the children so they can say and hear the rhymes. Once the children can recite the rhymes, show them the rhymes in a big book or written on a chart so that they can notice the print. Making nursery rhyme books using favorite rhymes gives children an opportunity to try to match pictures, rhymes, and print. Some children see the picture and remember the rhyme; other students pretend read the rhymes; and still others really read the rhymes by placing their fingers under each word and reading it, cross-checking with the letter sounds they know. Once again, what a child does with pictures and print depends upon what he or she knows and where the child is in his or her literacy development.

CENTERS

Kindergarten classrooms are famous for their centers—the play or dress up center, kitchen center, art center, writing center, reading center, science center, etc. **Learning Centers are an important part of a developmental kindergarten. It is in these centers that children explore and discover their environment individually or in small groups.** This book focuses on the centers where students practice reading, writing, and working with words—the Reading Center and the Writing Center.

Reading Center

The Reading Center should be a pleasant, cozy place. Some teachers use leftover furniture that has been donated to the classroom. Some schools buy child-size chairs and sofas, and other schools build reading lofts.

Important things to remember about the Reading Center:

1. The children should have a comfortable place to read alone or with a friend.

2. There should be lots of good books and other reading materials from which to choose.

Books which the teacher has read to the class are always favorites for the Reading Center, whether they are big books or little books. Books that contain "old favorites"—stories children have heard many times or books that have been read to many of them before they entered kindergarten—should also be included. Informational books and magazines should be available in the Reading Center as well as story books. As the school year progresses, class books and student-authored books can be added to the Reading Center.

Writing Center

A variety of writing materials (pencils, markers, pens, and crayons) and different kinds of paper (construction, newsprint, lined and unlined paper), should be available in the Writing Center. This first month, as students start school, they should be encouraged to copy from the boards and charts in the classroom: to write their own names and lists of other students' names, color words, and number words they find in the room. Also, they should be told it is all right to draw, pretend write (scribble) or **drite** (combination of drawing and writing) in the Writing Center. Children who have written at home will have no problem with this. Some children may feel they need permission to scribble or write as best they can. They get that permission when they see you model this or praise and display the work of students making their first attempts at writing. Most kindergarten students enjoy having envelopes in the center, too. This way they can deliver their message to a family member or a friend and feel "grown up." You may need to make rules for the students—no more than one envelope each time it is their turn to visit the Writing Center!

How Reading and Writing Centers are Multilevel

When children work in centers, they have an opportunity to learn through play. Some children get their first chance to hold a book and turn its pages in the Reading Center. This activity is an important part of learning to read. Some students pretend read to a class and show the pictures to an invisible audience, especially if this is the only way they have ever seen someone (a teacher) reading!

Other students look for their favorite book or a book on a topic about which they want to learn more (even if it is just "reading" the pictures). Still other students really read books or try to match the print in the book to the letters and sounds they already know.

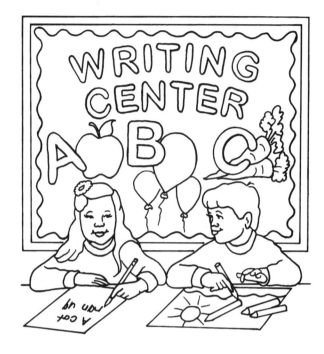

Some students have their first opportunities to write in the Writing Center because the writing instruments used in kindergarten (pencils, pens, markers, crayons, etc.) have not been available in their homes. Others need time to scribble and to pretend write as young children do. Finally, the ones who know what writing is and why we write have an opportunity to write for real reasons (messages, lists, copying from signs in the room, etc.). Reading and Writing Centers are multilevel by nature as children explore these special kindergarten places on their own.

16

OCTOBER

October is a busy month in kindergarten; there is so much to learn and so much to do! Many kindergarten classes are learning more about the students in the classroom by continuing with the "Getting to Know You" activity. Other kindergarten classes learn more about the school they attend by talking about special people within the school (the principal, art teacher, etc.). It is also time to focus some attention on the season, and fall is a wonderful time to learn about colors!

THE OPENING

- **"Who is here today?"**
- **"Is anyone absent?"**
- **"What day of the week is it?"**
- **"What is the month? date? year?"**
- **"How many days have we been in school? Can anyone count them? Let's make a mark (or tally mark) for each day."**

A straw is added to the jar. The straws have been grouped in bundles of ten and the children count along with you. They count the "tens" first, then the "ones" to find out how many days they have been in school. The new calendar for October is posted on a bulletin board where the students can see it and talk about the days of the week, the date, and chart the weather each day this month.

As the days progress and the calendar becomes more familiar, begin drawing the students' attention to the beginning of words. In particular, ask them to notice the beginning of the words they see on the calendar and bulletin board by using different, child-appropriate questions, such as

- **"How do you know this says Monday?**

- **"Can you find the word Monday on the calendar? What do you notice about the word Monday?"**

The answers vary depending upon which child you ask. Some answers include:

"It starts with an *M*."

"The word *day* is in it."

"*Monday* starts like *Michelle* or *Mom*."

The teacher then asks: "Who can point to the *M* in *Monday*? What day comes before *Monday*? What day will come after *Monday*? What do we usually do on Monday that is special?"

You may want to tell the class something that happened to you on the previous day; or you might want to let several students talk about their experiences. If there is a birthday or special day to talk about, it is done at this time. If the class is going to a special session/ class (Art, Music, P.E., or to the Library or Media Center or on a field trip), talk about it during the opening. Many teachers also share a favorite book, or books, on the current theme (fall or colors) at this time.

READING ALOUD TO CHILDREN

Kindergarten teachers need to read to children at least once every day, maybe more. It is all right to read a book to students just for the pleasure of hearing a good story. As you are reading to them, the children are developing some important language skills. Children need to learn how to listen, to think about the story and sequence of events, to try to predict what might happen, and to take turns answering questions about the story. While listening to the teacher read, kindergartners hear the sounds of letters and the sounds in words.

Young children also like to learn about new people and places. When you read informational books to the class, your students have an opportunity to learn while listening. Placing the books you read in the Reading Center gives children a chance to visit with the book again and again.

Favorite books for October:

Blueberries for Sal by Robert McCloskey (Viking Press, 1976).

Color Dance by Ann Jonas (Greenwillow Books, 1989).

Frederick by Leo Lionni (Alfred A. Knopf, Inc., 1967).

Green Eggs and Ham by Dr. Seuss (Random House, 1960).

Green Queen, The by Nick Sharratt (Candlewick Press, 1992).

Halloween by Miriam Nerlove (Albert Whitman,1989).

Harold and the Purple Crayon by Crockett Johnson (HarperCollins, 1955).

Haunted House by Bill Martin, Jr. (Holt, Rinehart, and Winston, 1970).

How Do Apples Grow? by Betsy Maestro (HarperCollins, 1993).

I See Colors by Rozanne Lanczak Williams (Creative Teaching Press, 1995).

I Went Walking by Sue Williams (Harcourt Brace, 1989).

Is It Red? Is It Yellow? Is It Blue? by Tana Hoban (Mulberry Books, 1978).

It's Pumpkin Time by Zoe Hall (Scholastic, Inc., 1994).

Johnny Appleseed by Steven Kellogg (Scholastic, Inc., 1988).

Little Red Hen pictures by Lucinda McQueen (Scholastic, Inc., 1985).

Polar Bear, Polar Bear, What Do You Hear? by Bill Martin, Jr. (Henry Holt & Co., 1991).

Seasons of Arnold's Apple Tree, The by Gail Gibbons (Harcourt Brace, 1988).

Trip, The by Ezra Jack Keats (Greenwillow Books, 1978).

White Is the Moon by Valerie Greeley (Macmillan, 1991).

White Rabbit's Color Book by Alan Baker (Kingfisher Books, 1994).

Who Said Red? by Mary Serfozo (Aladdin Books, 1992).

READING WITH CHILDREN—Shared Reading with Predictable Big Books

A favorite big book to read while learning about colors is *Brown Bear, Brown Bear, What Do You See?* by Bill Martin, Jr. (Holt, Rinehart, and Winston, 1967). It is a fun and easy way to learn about colors and color names as the children enjoy the book's repetitive pattern, pictures, and print.

Read and Talk About the Book

In the first and second reading of this book, focus on the meaning and enjoyment of the story. The book has delightful illustrations and children will enjoy finding out which animal will be used to illustrate each color. As you are reading the book, call attention to each color and the animal pictured for it. Are all ducks yellow? Are all dogs white? Are all (or any) elephants pink? The predictable text makes it easy for kindergarten students to chime in— and they do!

Encourage the Children to Join in the Reading

Once the children have picked up the repetition in the questions and responses, they will want to join in the reading. You might read the questions:

"Brown Bear, Brown Bear. What do you see?"

And let the children read the response:

"I see a Red Bird looking at me."

Or, divide the class in half and let each half take turns reading the questions and responses.

Act It Out

Brown Bear, Brown Bear, What Do You See? is a natural story for acting out. Let each student have a chance to be one of the characters. Use simple craft stick puppets or laminated, yarned picture card "necklaces" to act out the characters' parts.

Make the Book Available

Remember that children who have been read to want their favorite books read over and over. Then, they pretend they can read them, and they often actually do learn to read them. Be sure to put favorite big books and/or little book versions in the Reading Center for children to enjoy over and over. Add to the fun by putting audiotapes of the stories and props in the Listening Center so the students can act out the stories on their own!

WRITING WITH CHILDREN—
Shared Writing of Predictable Charts

Just as kindergarten classes enjoy reading predictable books together, they also like to write and read predictable charts. Writing a predictable chart is a natural follow-up to a predictable book or even a field trip or a new topic/theme. A predictable big book to use to begin writing predictable charts is *Things I Like* by Anthony Browne (Houghton Mifflin, 1996). It is the story of a little chimp who tells about all the things he likes ("This is me and this is what I like: Painting . . . and riding my bike. Playing with toys, and dressing up."). **The pictures in the book make it predictable, not the pattern!**

After reading and enjoying *Things I Like*, you and the children will make your own "Things I Like" chart. Begin by putting the title "Things I Like" on the top line of a large sheet of chart paper. As you write the title, say each word and the letters in each word so that children will watch both left to right progression and letter formation.

Next, write what you like to do, followed by your name in parentheses—"I like reading books." (Miss Williams). This is a model for the children to follow. Then, ask each child to tell something he or she likes or likes to do. Write their answers on the predictable chart and place each child's name after the sentence with parentheses around the name, separating it from the sentence.

This is what the finished chart might look like:

Things I Like

I like reading books. (Miss Williams)
I like swimming. (Michelle)
I like eating french fries. (Jasmine)
I like pizza. (Suzanne)
I like computers. (Ryan)
I like running. (Adam)
I like playing football. (Refugio)
I like riding my bike. (William)
I like playing basketball. (Erica)
I like making cookies. (Olivia)
I like going to the beach. (Mike)
I like making cookies. (Nikki)
I like watching TV. (Paul)
I like playing with my friends. (Mitchell)
I like soccer. (Jacob)
I like school. (Emily)
I like my Barbie dolls. (Julie)
I like going to the Mall. (Rashawn)
I like my teacher. (Tiara)
I like reading books. (Cindy)
I like drawing pictures. (Christopher)
I like Centers. (Paul)
I like computer games. (Mitchell)
I like school! (Richard)

When the predictable chart is completed, the teacher reads it to the children or has each child read his/her own sentence to the class. Kindergarten students can do this because they know each sentence starts with "I like. . ." and finishes with what they said. The predictability of the sentences on the chart helps all children to accomplish this task.

What Do You Notice?

On the following day, have the children read the predictable chart "Things I Like" again, with each child reading his/her own sentence. When you finish, ask the children to look at the sentences and come up and point to things they notice. **Children will notice a variety of things, depending upon what they know about letters, sounds, words, and reading.** Their observations may include:

All sentences begin with *I Like*.

French and *fries* begin with the same two letters—*fr*.

Ryan and *Refugio* both start with an *R*.

I is at the beginning of each sentence!

I is always a capital (or big) letter!

Lots of words have *ing* at the end.

TV is spelled with two letters, *T* and *V*.

All sentences have this (a period) at the end.

Whatever the children notice is accepted and praised by the teacher. The teacher points to the chart and asks more questions—"Does anyone know what this mark is called? Why is it placed there?"— and offers explanations: "That is called an exclamation point. It is placed there to show that the teacher really likes her class and is excited about them." "Good noticing! TV is made up of two letters. Does anyone know what kind of letters those are?" Another activity the children like to do is to "act out" their sentence. By reading the names on the chart the children will know whose turn is next.

Sentence Builders

• Write the first sentence from the chart on a sentence strip with a thick black magic marker.

• Have a child find the first sentence on the chart and match the sentence strip to it.

• Do this for several of the sentences on your predictable chart.

• Let the children watch as you cut the first sentence into words, one word at a time.

• Mix up the words for this sentence and have the students use the words to recreate the sentence, just as it is written on the first line of your predictable chart.

• Let the children become sentence builders. Choose one child for each word in the sentence and give each child a word card. If you are using Emily's sentence from the chart, let Emily "be" her name at the end of the sentence. Let the children stand in front of the class in the same order as the words in the first sentence on the chart.

- Read the sentence aloud *after* the children get in place where each child thinks he or she belongs.

- Some children will check the chart, then get in the right place; other children will not only find their place quickly, but also will help any child who does not automatically get in the right spot!

Repeat this procedure for the second sentence, taking the words and giving those words to different children. Ask the students to become "sentence builders" and to get in the right order, so that they look like the second sentence on the chart. When the children get in their places, read the sentence, so that the children can see if they have completed the task correctly. Let every child "be" a word during this activity.

Making a Class Book

The final activity for each predictable chart is creating a **class book**. Have the children reread the predictable chart again, then give each child an envelope with his/her cutup sentence inside. Have each child sequence the words to make the sentence on the bottom of a piece of drawing paper. Check the sentences to see if they are correct, then the children can tape or paste the words in their sentence on the paper. Next, the children can illustrate their sentences using colored markers or crayons. Put these pages together into a class book which you and the children read together. Kindergarten children enjoy seeing their own work, and their classmates' work, turned into a book.

How Writing a Predictable Chart is Multilevel

Cutting sentences into words and rearranging them, having the children "be" the words, and making new sentences from familiar words help students understand what words are. When writing a predictable chart, there are many different things for young children to notice. Children with little print experience learn what reading is and begin to develop "print concepts." They learn that each sentence starts at the left and goes to the right. They see the teacher start at the top of the page and go to the bottom. They hear the teacher talk about "words," "sentences," and "letters" and learn about these things. Those children who come to kindergarten already reading can usually read the whole chart and further their reading skills as they learn more words and the similarities and differences between them.

GETTING TO KNOW YOU

The "Getting to Know You" activity is not usually completed in the first month of school. Teachers continue the process of picking names, interviewing children, cheering for each child, writing each child's name, and having the class draw pictures of each "Special Student." When you are past the halfway point in adding the names to the bulletin board, let the students take charge of noticing the similarities and differences between the names. Instead of pointing out that Robert's name starts with the same letter and letter sound as Ryan, say "What do you notice about the letters and sounds in Robert's name and the other names on our bulletin board?"

Another activity you can do with children's names is to "clap" the syllables in words. This will help students develop the phonemic awareness ability to segment words into syllables. Pick a name and say the name, "clapping" the syllables as you say it. Then, say the name again, having the children clap with you. The term **syllables** may be difficult for most young children to understand, so you may want to refer to the syllables as *beats*. Children should realize by clapping that *Mike* is a one-beat word, *Jasmine* is a two-beat word, and *Refugio* is a four-beat word.

There is a system and a pattern in the way letters represent sounds. Our instruction should point out these patterns. Children who see a new word, and ask themselves how that new word is like the other words they know, can discover many patterns on their own. "Getting to Know You" is not just to get to know the other students, but also to learn about letter/sound relationships in a way that makes sense to young children.

DEVELOPING PHONEMIC AWARENESS— Rhymes, Chants, and Rhyming Books

Have you listened to kindergartners on the playground when they want to tease one another? What do they say? Often, you hear chants such as "Silly Billy," "Saggy, baggy Maggie," and "Susie Pusie!" The children are becoming aware of words and sounds and can manipulate these to express themselves—and to impress others! **Children and rhymes just go together. Children love to chant, sing, and make up rhymes!**

Most kindergarten teachers have an amazing store of rhymes and fingerplays to go with their units throughout the seasons. For example: "One, Two Buckle My Shoe" when learning to count and "Five Little Pumpkins" for October. Doing rhymes with children, however, is not just for fun! **Rhyming activities develop one of the most critical concepts for success in beginning reading— phonemic awareness.** Children like to chant rhymes and do any fingerplays that go along with the words. Rhyming allows children to listen to the words and learn more about words and how they work.

Remember the little girl Michelle, whose favorite book was *In A People House*? She developed phonemic awareness by the time she was three. At that time, she had imaginary friends whom she named Eedie, Beedie, and Deedie. Michelle had learned how to manipulate letters and sounds to make new names— she was ready for letter-sound instruction (phonics) long before she went to school.

Most children who come to school with well-developed phonemic awareness abilities have been read lots of Dr. Seuss books. Wanting to simulate what happens in literate homes before children come to school, kindergarten teachers develop phonemic awareness by using such Dr. Seuss books as *Hop on Pop* (Random House, 1963); *One Fish, Two Fish, Red Fish, Blue Fish* (Random House, 1966); *The Foot Book* (Random House, 1968); *The Ear Book* (Random House, 1968); and *There's a Wocket in My Pocket* (Random House, 1974).

Another rhyming (big) book that kindergartners love is *Golden Bear* by Ruth Young (Puffin Books, 1992). It is the story of an adorable African-American boy and his teddy bear. The boy sees his bear everywhere: on a stair and in a chair; playing a violin under his chin; on a rug with a bug; and on the ice making circles twice.

After reading and rereading this book, help the children come up with some other rhyming places Golden Bear might be found. Can the bear be found in the park after dark, or in school being cool, or in the car with a jar?

Rhymes are not just to read—rhymes are to have fun with! As kindergarten children participate in shared reading and writing, they become aware of words as separate entities. **Using fingerplays with rhyming words, reading rhyming books, and talking about rhyming words give all children a chance to increase their phonemic awareness.**

Making up rhymes and playing with words is one of the most reliable indicators that children are getting control of language.

CENTERS

It is October, so fall, colors, and Halloween are the topics of learning in the centers this month. (Using Halloween as a topic depends upon where you live and the parents of the children you teach!)

Reading Center

The Reading Center is filled with books on these topics. Some books have been read to the class; some have not. The Reading Center gives children at all levels of learning a chance to hold the books and to see the words and pictures about the themes they are discussing. **Some kindergarten students will look at pictures and learn, other students will "pretend read" and learn, and the ones who can already read will "really read" the books and become even more fluent at reading.**

Writing Center

The Writing Center walls are filled with charts—charts for both color words and fall words. One activity the students can make while in the Writing Center is an "October Pictionary" using the words from the charts or bulletin board. **Some children will copy the words from the various charts on pieces of paper and draw pictures to match the words. Other children will use the pencils, markers, and crayons in the center to scribble, draw, "drite," and write the words depending upon where they are in their writing development.** At the end of the activity, staple together each student's pages so that every student will have a little book he or she can take home.

Since entering kindergarten, most children have learned more about writing and more about how to write. They enjoy the Writing Center because it is a place where they can practice what they have learned and where their efforts will be rewarded with a smile and kind words.

NOVEMBER

November is the month when teachers realize that although the students have finally settled into the daily routine of kindergarten, the holidays will be here soon! From this point forward, it seems as if there is never enough time for teachers to do everything they want to do and read every book they want to read. In this chapter we will once again focus on learning more about letters, sounds, and words by shared reading and writing. Discussing Thanksgiving and all the things for which we are thankful take up a big part of November. Some teachers use the Thanksgiving holiday to study families and how families have changed over time. Some teachers also use this time before the annual Thanksgiving feast to learn about food, the food groups, and nutrition.

THE OPENING

The opening has become routine, and all the students have had time to listen and become familiar with these procedures. The students know what will be talked about each morning and are comfortable with the usual questions about the calendar, days of the week, the date, the month, the seasons, and the various types of weather they have encountered since school began. They are willing to take turns talking and answering questions during the opening. When asked, "What do you notice?" about a particular sentence or group of words, the students' answers show their growth in letter, letter sound, and word knowledge. You have been working hard to teach these concepts and your efforts are paying off. For this, you are thankful!

READING ALOUD TO CHILDREN

November is a good month to read both stories and new informational books about a variety of subjects.

When learning about families, there are many books you can read to your students. *Alexander and the Terrible, Horrible, No Good, Very Bad Day* by Judith Viorst (Aladdin Books, 1972) is a wonderful story about a traditional family. All children (and adults!) relate to this story because we have all had days like that! If you want to read about a family from long ago, then read *Ox-Cart Man* by Donald Hall (Viking Press, 1979) and talk about "the olden days." Another, more recent, book by Judith Viorst is *Alexander, Who's Not (Do You Hear Me? I Mean It!) Going to Move* (Atheneum Books, 1995) about a family that is moving, and a little boy who does not want to move. For classes that have children who have recently moved or have someone who will be moving soon, this is a good book to read.

For those who have extended families, do not forget the stories Tomie De Paola writes about his grandmothers, *Nana Upstairs, Nana Downstairs* about his Irish grandmother (Puffin Books,1978) and *Watch Out For Chicken Feet in My Soup* about his Italian grandmother (Puffin Books, 1974). *The Song and Dance Man* by Karen Ackerman (Scholastic, Inc., 1988) is the wonderful story of a grandfather with a colorful past.

Many students can relate to the book *The Relatives Came* by Cynthia Rylant (Scholastic, Inc., 1985). Another book you may want to read with your students is *The Night Before Christmas* by Clement C. Moore (American Greeting Co., 1976). While reading these books, your students may want to talk about their mothers, fathers, sisters, brothers, grandparents, and anyone with whom they live or whom they love. To help young children learn about changing families, *Dinosaurs Divorce: A Guide for Changing Families* by Laurene and Marc Brown (Little, 1986) is a good book to read.

Stories to add a multicultural aspect to your classroom are *"More More More," Said the Baby: Three Love Stories* by Vera B. Williams (Scholastic, Inc., 1990); *Everett Anderson's Nine Month Long* by Lucille Clifton (Henry Holt & Co., 1978); *A Chair For My Mother* by Vera B. Williams (Wm. Morrow, 1984); and *Mama, Do You Love Me?* by Barbara M. Joosse (Chronicle Books, 1991). *Mama, Do You Love Me?* is about an Inuit child who discovers her mother's love for her to be unconditional. *Just Like Daddy* by Frank Asch (Aladdin Books, 1981) is a story about a little bear who tries to be like his dad from the start of the day until he catches a fish—just like Mommy!

When studying about food and how we need good food to grow, there are many wonderful books to read. *Growing Vegetable Soup* by Lois Ehlert (Harcourt Brace, 1987) is one such book. After reading this book, you can plan to "grow" some vegetable soup of your own. Parents can be invited to share this simple "Thanksgiving feast" at school. While planning and writing the menu, you have another opportunity to call attention to letters and sounds as well as words. What will we put in

our soup? Carrots, green beans, tomatoes, onions, corn, peas, and potatoes are some good choices. How can we sort the vegetables we are putting in our soup? Which of those vegetable names begin alike? Which of the vegetables are the same color? Kindergarten children enjoy learning through reading—just like adults!

Informational books to read in November:

Enormous Watermelon, The retold by Brenda Parkes and Judith Smith (Rigby, 1986).

Growing Colors by Bruce McMillan (Lothrop, Lee, and Shepard Books, 1988).

Molly's Pilgrim by Barbara Cohen (Bantam-Doubleday, 1995).

One Tough Turkey by Steven Kroll (Holiday House, 1982).

Popcorn Book by Tomie De Paola (Scholastic, Inc., 1987).

Thanksgiving Day by Gail Gibbons (Holiday House, 1984).

Today Is Thanksgiving! by P. K. Hallinan (Ideal's Children Books, 1993).

What Is Thanksgiving? by Harriet Ziefert (HarperCollins, 1992).

READING WITH CHILDREN— Shared Reading with Predictable Books

Some books, such as *Things I Like* (previously cited) are predictable because of the pictures. Other books, such as *Brown Bear, Brown Bear* (previously cited) have predictable patterns. Still other books have both predictable pictures and text, such as *Little Red Hen* (previously cited). Byron Barton's beautifully illustrated retelling of the well-known tale was selected for this activity; you might choose a version by Paul Galdone, Margot Zemarch, or Patricia and Frederick McKissack. In Barton's version, the little red hen's friends would rather play than work. When the hen asks who will help her plant seeds, cut the stalks, thresh the wheat, grind the grain, and make flour into bread, her friends repeatedly reply, "Not I." But they have a different answer when she asks who will help eat the bread she has made!

This is a wonderful book for shared reading in kindergarten. **The story is predictable, it does not have too much print, and the sentence patterns are very repetitious. The pictures support the familiar sentence patterns. The story also appeals to children because they have all said "Not I" at some time or other—or wanted to!** A teacher can read this book during November and can tie into family, food, or Thanksgiving themes.

Read, Discuss, and Reread the Book

The first time you read the book to your class, let them just listen to the story and enjoy it. You may want to reread this story and talk about what the little red hen does when she finds some seeds—and why. This will help the students understand the steps involved in turning wheat into flour and will also set the mood for the story. The third time you read the story the children will want to join in; they know the answer each time will be "Not I."

Act It Out

Your class will definitely want to act out this story! Let several children become the characters (they do not need costumes to pretend) and "act out" the story as you reread it again. Another way to "act out" the story is to make yarned cards, worn like necklaces, or animal puppets. You can make simple animal puppets by gluing small drawings of the animals to popsicle or craft sticks. Reread the story several times, giving different children a chance to be the characters. Young children love acting out this story and saying, "Not I." By rereading the story again and again, the children become familiar with the story and can then read or pretend read the book.

What Do You Notice?

Read each page in the big book again, stopping to talk about what the students notice about the print. Some responses you may hear include:

"There is a lot of *Not I*."

"*Cat* and *cut* begin with *c*."

"*Cat*, *pig*, and *hen* have just 3 letters!"

"*Day* and *duck* start with *d*."

"*Me* and *make* both start with the *m* sound like *Michelle*."

Ask the children about the quotation marks if they do not mention them. Not all children are ready to learn about quotation marks, but some are, and pointing them out makes it a more multilevel activity.

WRITING WITH CHILDREN— Shared Writing with Predictable Charts

After reading the *Little Red Hen* (previously cited), you might want to make a predictable chart about how your kindergarten students like to help people (I like to help . . .). Following a story about the first Thanksgiving or Thanksgiving today, it is easy to write another predictable chart by talking about the things for which the students are thankful. Start with a big piece of chart paper and write the title "I Am Thankful For..." at the top of the page.

As you listen to the things for which five-year-olds are thankful, you realize that the little things in life mean big things to these youngsters. As each child tells something for which he or she is thankful, write it on the chart, followed by the child's name in parentheses. On the last line (or the first line), write something for which you are thankful.

I Am Thankful For...

I am thankful for my mommy. (Adam)

I am thankful for my sister. (Michelle)

I am thankful for french fries. (Jasmine)

I am thankful for my Teddy Bear. (Erica)

I am thankful for Tommy, my cat. (Suzanne)

I am thankful for my dog. (Ryan)

I am thankful for school. (Refugio)

I am thankful for food. (William)

I am thankful for turkey. (Mike)

I am thankful for my friends. (Olivia)

I am thankful for my daddy. (Jacob)

I am thankful for my family. (Emily)

I am thankful for my home. (Mitchell)

I am thankful for my grandma. (Nikki)

I am thankful for everything! (Paul)

I am thankful for my teacher. (Tiara)

I am thankful for good food. (Julie)

I am thankful for my nana and grampy. (Jimmy)

I am thankful for my new house. (Rashawn)

I am thankful for my trailer. (Christopher)

I am thankful for my class! (Miss Williams)

When you have finished the shared writing of this predictable chart, read the chart from beginning to end with the students. The next day, the students are ready to read their own sentences, alone or with help, and talk about the things they notice. Several students are quick to point out that *mommy*, *my*, and *Michelle* start with *M*. Some children know that *teddy*, *teacher*, and *Tommy* begin with the same letter and sound. Another child may notice *Thanksgiving* begins with the same letter but does not have the same beginning sound as *Tommy* and *Teddy*. Many students can read the words "I am Thankful For . . ." at the beginning of the chart and each sentence without any help at all from you. Most children know the ending mark after each sentence is a period—some students even know why you put it there!

Some other books to use for making predictable charts in November are:

How Can I Help? by Christine Hood (Creative Teaching Press, 1996).

I Am Special by Kimberly Jordano (Creative Teaching Press, 1996).

Look What I Can Do by Jose Aruego (Aladdin Books, 1971).

Saturday Mornings by Joelie Hancock (Mondo, 1995).

We Can Share at School by Rozanne Lanczak Williams (Creative Teaching Press, 1996).

Sentence Builders

The following day, the children will read the predictable chart again and become sentence builders. Kindergarten children love to get in front of the class and make or build the sentences on the chart with the words that you have given them. After the students build the sentence, read the sentence aloud to the class to check that the students are in the right order. Let the children build several of the sentences from the predictable chart, then call attention to some letters, sounds, or words which you want to discuss.

What Do You Notice?

To focus some attention on beginning letters and sounds, some teachers have the class go on an "M Hunt" and find *M* words on the chart. Or, the teacher may ask the students to find all the words on the chart that begin with *D*, like David. It is a more multilevel approach to ask, "What do you notice?" That question stretches the children who know letters and sound relationships, as well as those who are not aware of them yet.

Making A Class Book

On the fourth day, the children will place and paste down their cutup sentence onto a piece of drawing paper. Once this is done, the children will illustrate their sentences with crayons or markers. Every student will have a page in the new class book, "I am Thankful For..." which will go in the Reading Center where all students can read and enjoy it again and again!

WRITING FOR CHILDREN— Journal Writing

A wonderful way to begin journal writing is to end each day by talking about what your kindergarten class did that day and then to write about it while the students watch you. The first thing you do is write the date. Next, discuss the events of the day. You may need to help the students organize the events in the correct order and decide about what to write (you cannot write every detail of every day). Then, write these sentences on a large piece of chart paper.

November 2

Today we began school with big group. Next, we heard a story. Then, we made a page for our class book about our families. We went to P.E. with Mr. Sikes. After P.E., we did Math. We ended our day with centers.

As you write, talk about what you are doing and why.

"My first sentence is about the first thing we did today."

"I start each sentence with a capital letter because sentences begin that way."

Writing a journal entry at the end of each day helps students focus on the important things they did in school that day. To get your students ready to spell words, model this for them daily during your journal entry. When you begin words like *made* or *Math,* you can say, "This word begins like *Michelle* (or *McDonalds®*). We know that words which begin like *Michelle* begin with *m.*" Stretch out the words as you say and spell them so the children can hear the sounds and then watch as you write the letter(s).

When you write for children, you provide a model for them. Later, when they are asked to write their own journal entries each day, they will know what is expected and how to do it.

GETTING TO KNOW YOU— Connecting Children's Names to Letters and Sounds

By the end of November, everyone in the class will have had a chance to be the spotlight child, to take home the pictures their classmates have drawn of them, and to have their names put up on the "Special Student" bulletin board. Another class-made book, "Our Class," is in the Reading Center, and some of your students can read all of the names.

There are two kinds of learning based on your brain's two types of memory stores. Things we just "do over and over" until we learn them are put in our **rote memory store. This rote-memory store has a limited capacity, and if we do not practice something that is contained in rote memory for a while, then the rote memory gives that information's space to something more current.** (What was her phone number? Before she went to Florida, I called her every day and knew it, but now I will have to look it up again!) **The other memory store, the associative store, has unlimited capacity. We can find things in the associative memory store that we have not thought about for years if the memory is triggered by the right image, smell, or song, etc. The trick to putting information in the associative store rather than in the rote store is that you have to make an association about the information.**

Children who are trying to remember that a particular shape turned a particular way is called *d,* and that it has the sound we hear in *doughnut* and *dog*, cannot make associations between the name and sound of *d* with *doughnut* and *dog* unless they can **read** the words *doughnut* and *dog*! These children may just try to remember that it is called *d*, and it has the sound of *doughnut* and *dog*. They put all this information into their rote-memory stores, and if they do not use it for a while (such as when they go home for two weeks at Christmas!), the space in their rote memory will be used up by something else. Then, the students will have to learn the letter and sound information over again!

The only way to help children put letter name and sound knowledge in their associative stores rather than their rote stores is to make sure they can read some words which contain the letters. If all the student names are on your "Special Student" bulletin board, you can now use these names as associative links to letter names and sounds.

Imagine that the names of the children displayed on the bulletin board are:

Jasmine	Ryan	Michelle
Mike	Adam	Erica
Suzanne	Refugio	William
Olivia	Jacob	Emily
Mitchell	Nikki	Paul
Tiara	Julie	Jimmy
Rashawn	Christopher	

Write down each student's name on a card or sentence strip and pass them out to the students. **Begin the activity with a letter that many children have in their names and that usually has its expected sound.** With this class, you might begin with the letter *r*. Have all children whose names have an *r* in them come to the front of the class, holding the card or sentence strip with their names. First, count all the *r*'s. There are seven *r*'s in all. Next, have the children whose names contain an *r* to divide themselves into those whose names begin with an *r* (Ryan, Rashawn, and Refugio), those whose names end with an *r* (Christopher), and those with an *r* in their names that is not the first or the last letter (Erica, Tiara). Finally, say each name slowly—stretching out the letters—and decide if you can hear the usual sound of that letter. For *r*, you can hear the usual sound in all of these names.

Now, choose another letter and let those children come to the front of the room and display their name cards. Count the number of times the letter occurs, and then have the children divide themselves into groups according to whether the letter is the first letter in their names, the last letter, or in between. Finally, say the names—stretching them out—and decide if you can hear the usual sound that the letter makes. The letter *m* would be a good

second choice for this list of names. You would have Michelle and Mike beginning with *m*, Adam and William ending with *m*, and Jasmine, Emily, and Jimmy having an *m* that is not the first or last letter. Again, you can hear the usual sound of *m* in all these names.

Continue picking letters and having children come to the front of the classroom with their name cards. Do not try to do all the letters, just those that are represented in several names.

DEVELOPING PHONEMIC AWARENESS— Rhyming Books

Most young children who have been read to can hear rhyme, and often ask the reader to reread the page or to repeat the rhyme. Many of us remember nursery rhymes we learned them by heart because we heard them so many times! We also noticed the rhyming words at the end of a line. Dr. Seuss's Beginner Books are like that—young children cannot help but hear the rhyme. Often, as we read these books to them, children begin to guess the next rhyming word because they are paying such close attention to both the pictures and print.

One example of a book where students cannot help but notice the rhyme is Dr. Seuss's *Green Eggs and Ham* (Random House, 1960). It is about a character named Sam-I-am and eating green eggs and ham. The first reading is always just for the pleasure of hearing the story. From the very first page, students listen to the words and begin to hear the rhyme. After several pages, even children without much print experience can hear the rhyming words: "I do not like them in a house. I do not like them with a mouse. I do not like them here or there. I do not like them anywhere. I do not like green eggs and ham. I do not like them, Sam-I-am." After reading the story and talking about it, reread it and find the rhyming words. The rhymes repeat several times which make pairs of rhyming words easy to spot.

Favorite Rhyming Books:

ABC Rhymes illustrated by R. W. Alley (D. C. Heath, 1991).

Annie Bananie by Leah Komaiko (Scholastic, Inc.,1987).

Ape in a Cape: An Alphabet of Odd Animals by Fritz Eichenberg (Harcourt Brace, 1952).

Bears in Pairs by Niki Yektai (MacMillan, 1987).

Bug in a Jug and Other Funny Rhymes, A by Gloria Patrick (D.C. Heath, 1993).

Each Peach Pear Plum by Janet and Allan Ahlberg (Viking Press, 1978).

Everett Anderson's Nine Month Long by Lucille Clifton (Henry Holt & Co., 1978).

Golden Bear by Ruth Young (Puffin Books, 1992).

Hop on Pop by Dr. Seuss (Random House, 1963).

Jake Baked the Cake by B. G. Hennessey (Viking Press, 1990).

Monkeys in the Jungle by Angie Sage (Houghton Mifflin, 1991).

One Fish, Two Fish, Red Fish, Blue Fish by Dr. Seuss (Random House, 1966).

Pretend You're a Cat by J. Marzollo (Dial Books, 1990).

CENTERS

Reading Center

November is here and the Reading Center contains many new books about the Thanksgiving holiday and families. It also contains books that the class has made. Children are reading these books by themselves and to a friend when they are in the Reading Center. Some children try to read newspapers and magazines just as they have seen grown-ups do. Often, they pretend they are the teacher and share a book they can read just like the teacher does in class—they read the text first and then show the pictures.

Writing Center

The Writing Center has a new November Pictionary chart or bulletin board on the wall. There is also another chart for the children to look at with pictures and names of people, places, and events from the first Thanksgiving. Children find new Thanksgiving-themed rubber stamps and an ink pad in the Writing Center to use during November. They can stamp a Pilgrim on a piece of paper and write the word *pilgrim* with it, if they wish. There are stamps with a turkey, a pumpkin, an Indian, and food to be used by the children when writing in the center. Many students will draw and write using the stamps. Others will use the stamps to create pictures, then color and decorate these pictures. Some kindergarten students write the things for which they are thankful, just like the teacher does in class. With stamps, pictures, and print, the students get their messages down on paper. When you listen to, look at, and praise these early attempts at writing, the students are pleased with themselves and begin to see themselves as writers.

December is always a busy month—both at home and at school! The holidays (Christmas, Hanukkah, and Kwanzaa) are almost here, and you can use the children's interest and enthusiasm for these upcoming events to do more reading, writing, and working with words.

THE OPENING

The Opening is a time when kindergarten classes have a chance to discuss this busy month! The children are well aware of the opening routine by now, and their excitement for the season may show during the opening. They may notice that *Santa* starts like *Saturday* and *Sunday* and *Merry* starts like *Monday*! Some students may even notice that Christmas, Kwanzaa and Hanukkah all start with capital (big) letters. Talking about the upcoming holidays fills the opening each morning, as do all the stories and books that teachers want to share with their students. Teachers and students look at the calendar and count down the days until vacation begins.

READING ALOUD TO CHILDREN

Reading to children about the holidays capitalizes on their enthusiasm for the season and helps to calm them as they sit quietly while you read to them in "big group." Activities in centers can focus on the stories you read or on the holidays and ideas about which the students are learning.

There are many multicultural books now available to read to youngsters, so children can learn about many different holidays and the way people celebrate in different parts of the country and the world.

Books about holidays and celebrations:

Christmas Time by Gail Gibbons (Holiday House, 1982).

Corduroy's Christmas by B. G. Hennessy (Viking Press, 1992).

Hanukkah by Gail Gibbons (Holiday House, 1986).

Kwanzaa by Gail Gibbons (Holiday House, 1986).

Mr. Willowby's Christmas Tree by Robert Barry (McGraw Hill, 1963).

Nine Days to Christmas by Marie Hall Ets (Puffin Books, 1991).

Too Many Tamales by Gary Soto (Scholastic, Inc., 1993).

'Twas the Night Before Christmas in the Desert by Charlotte Van Bebber (Doe Eyes Publ., 1984).

What Is Christmas? by Lillie James (HarperCollins, 1994).

When Will Santa Come? by Harriet Ziefert (HarperCollins, 1991).

READING WITH CHILDREN— Shared Reading with Predictable Big Books

Goodnight Moon by Margaret Wise Brown (Scholastic, 1989) is a bedtime favorite. With its repetition, rhyme, and pictures that support the print, this story is a perfect choice for shared reading. In the story, a little rabbit tries to prolong bedtime by saying "goodnight" to everything in sight. The story is also a rhythmic review of color words and rhyming words as well. Listen to the beginning words,

In the great green room

There was a telephone

And a red balloon

And a picture of —

The cow jumping over the moon.

Young children may recognize the bunny's technique as one they use to avoid going to sleep until they, like the bunny, cannot keep their eyes open another minute! Read the book and enjoy the story. Then, reread the story. After you read each page, ask the children to point out objects that are mentioned in the text. "Where is the balloon in this picture?" This is good vocabulary development for your students as they learn the names of objects that may be found in their own homes. Reread the story a third time and talk about the rhyming words.

Encourage Children to Join In the Reading

On the fourth reading of the story, have your kindergarten students "share" the reading by saying the rhyming words.

Teacher: "The cow jumping over the—"

Students: "moon."

Teacher: "And there were three little bears sitting on—"

Students: "chairs."

Teacher: "And two little kittens And a pair of—"

Students: "mittens."

The pictures will help the students to finish each sentence, but they must think of what rhymes as well. There are socks in the picture as well as mittens, so ask, "Why didn't you say socks?" The students should be able to answer that socks did not rhyme. You may want to have students read this story with you more than once. Let them try to read along with you now that they know the story and the words in the story. The pictures and rhymes on the pages will help many children to accomplish this task.

What Do You Notice?

Open to a page in the middle of the book and ask students what they notice about the words (print).

> Goodnight light
> Goodnight clocks
>
> And the red balloon
> Goodnight socks
>
> Goodnight bears
> Goodnight chairs

You may hear the students say things like

> "There are a lot of *goodnights*!" (five)

> "*Goodnight* is one word, but it sounds like two words."

> "*Clock* and *sock* rhyme and look alike at the end."

> "I see the word *red*."

> "*Bears* and *chairs* rhyme, but do not look alike."

> "*Bear* and *balloon* start with a *b*."

You could follow-up this story by writing a predictable chart. Ask each child for another "Goodnight—" line that he or she would use if it were bedtime at home. *Goodnight Moon* has endless possibilities. It is a super story for shared reading at this time of year when children may have trouble going to sleep because they are anticipating the holidays.

WRITING WITH CHILDREN—Shared Writing with Predictable Charts

After discussing the upcoming holidays in December (be sure to include all the special days that students in your school population may celebrate), you are ready to begin writing a predictable chart on a large piece of lined paper. A predictable chart that kindergarten children love to write during this season is titled "For the Holidays" and consists of the repeating sentence: "I want ...." Each child tells the one thing that he or she wants most during the holiday season. After writing each child's response, write his or her name after the sentence in parentheses. When all the children have contributed a sentence, let each child read his or her own sentence aloud.

> For the Holidays
>
> I want a basketball. (Mike)
>
> I want a bear. (Jasmine)
>
> I want a computer. (Ryan)
>
> I want a book. (Adam)
>
> I want a Panthers' jacket. (Adam J.)
>
> I want a video game. (Olivia)
>
> I want a bike. (Michelle)
>
> I want rollerblades. (Emily)
>
> I want to see my Grandma. (Refugio)
>
> I want an airplane. (Paul)
>
> I want peace in the world. (Jacob)

What Do You Notice?

On the second day, the holiday predictable chart is reread by the teacher. Then, each child reads his or her own sentence. Ask the children to look at these sentences and point out what they notice about the words and sentences on the chart. Children will notice a variety of things depending on their level of development, such as

"All sentences begin with an *I want*."

"*I* is always a capital (or big) letter!"

"*Basketball*, *book*, *bear*, and *bike* begin with the same letter *B*."

"*Ryan* and *Refugio* start with an *R*."

"Most of the kids want toys."

"All sentences have a period at the end."

Accept and praise whatever the children notice. Ask more questions, such as, "Can anyone find any other words that begin with *R*? Why is there a period at the end of each sentence?"

Sentence Builders

On the third day, write the first sentence from the predictable chart on a sentence strip with a thick black magic marker. Have a child find the first sentence on the chart and match the sentence strip to it. Do this for several of the sentences on your predictable chart. Next, let the children watch as you cut the first sentence strip into words, one word at a time. Mix up the words for the sentence and have students recreate the sentence just as it is written on the first line of your chart. Then, let the children become sentence builders. Give each child a word —include the child whose sentence is being built each time and give them their own

name. Ask students to stand in front of the class in the right order so that they look like the sentence on the chart. Some children will check the chart, then get in their places; others will not only find their places quickly, but help any child who does not automatically get in the right spot. Read the sentence aloud after the children get where they think they belong so the other students can check to see if the sentence builders completed the task correctly. Repeat this sentence building procedure for each sentence on the chart.

Making A Class Book

On the fourth day, the children can reread the predictable chart again. Write each sentence on a sentence strip, cut into words, and give to the students. Give each student his or her own sentence from the chart. Let each child arrange his or her cutup sentence on the bottom of a piece of drawing paper. After you check the sentences, the children can paste the words on the paper. Next, the children can take crayons or colored markers and illustrate their sentences. These pages are then put together into a class big book. Read the class book aloud on the fifth and final day before adding it to the Reading Center.

WRITING FOR CHILDREN—
Journal Writing

Continue to write a journal entry for the children each day in December. It will help your young students keep track of what happens each day and the many different multicultural events about which they learn. Journal writing is also a good way to remind students of upcoming events and things they need to bring to school from home. As you write, tell the students what you are doing and why. Ask questions: "What letter do I need to write at the beginning of the word *Hanukkah*? What are some things we have learned about Hanukkah? What toy did we play with today? What sounds do you hear in that word? Let's stretch it out and listen."

Children need to know how people think as they write. It will help the students when they are in the Writing Center and when you ask them to write later in the year.

Morning Message

So many things happen each day during December that it is a good time to begin writing a **morning message** on the board. The morning message is another way to write for children. Write a morning message to tell students about the day. Many teachers do this as a part of the opening. Other teachers do it when they call the big group together for shared reading.

The first morning message could be something like

> Dear Class,
>
> Today is Monday, December 2.
>
> I have a new book to read today.
>
> Love,
>
> Miss Williams

The next day, write:

> Dear Class,
>
> Yesterday, we read a new book.
>
> Today, we will make patterns.
>
> Love,
>
> Miss Williams

Each day, write a message to your class, and each day the students can watch you write. Read the message together and talk about what it "says" and what will happen that day. Finally, have the children count as you record the number of words in each sentence and then the number of letters in each sentence.

From these experiences, children will be learning the **jargon** of print. Jargon refers to all the words we use to talk about reading and writing, and includes terms such as **word**, **letter**, **sentence**, and **sound**.

How Writing for Children is Multilevel

Some children see what writing is and how to write, perhaps for the first time, during shared writing activities. Other children learn that writing goes from left to right and top to bottom on the page, because they watch what you do when you write. Still other children learn about letters and sounds as you stretch out the pronunciation of some words and they see you write a letter as they hear the sound. Finally, those bright and early readers are really reading the morning message and learning to spell some new words!

DEVELOPING PHONEMIC AWARENESS— Rhyming Books

A favorite story at this time of year is *The Night Before Christmas* by Clement C. Moore (previously cited). The whole story is written in rhyme. After reading the story several times, have the children listen for the rhyming words. Maybe the students can jingle a bell each time they hear a rhyming word! Or, perhaps you can read the story again but leave off the word that rhymes and see if your students can figure out what the word is.

Teacher: "'Twas the night before Christmas when all through the house.
Not a creature was stirring not even a —"

Students: "mouse."

Teacher: "The stockings were hung by the chimney with care.
In hopes that Saint Nicholas soon would be—"

Students: "there."

Teacher: The children were nestled all snug in their beds.
While visions of sugar plums danced in their —"

Students: "heads."

There are other holiday songs (*Rudolph*, *Jingle Bells*, *Silent Night*, etc.), stories, and fingerplays that will help children learn about rhyming words. Take the opportunity to point out the rhyming words as your students enjoy these activities.

CENTERS

Reading Center

The Reading Center is filled with books about the holidays. Many children are trying to read *The Night Before Christmas* (previously cited) because they have heard it so many times. They can predict what is coming next in the story and use the pictures and letters they see at the beginning of words to figure out the text. **This is a good time to add catalogs to the Reading Center. Children soon learn how to find what they are wishing for in these books that are full of both pictures and print.** Catalogs are also plentiful at holiday time, but if you do not have enough to bring to school for the Reading Center, ask parents or stores in the community to donate several to your classroom.

Writing Center

The Writing Center is filled with holiday words and pictures. The crayons, markers, pencils, pens, and a new set of holiday stamps are familiar to all students by this time of the year. Some children are ready to make their December Pictionary. Other children are trying to write letters to Santa Claus using pictures and what they know about print. Children have plenty to say at this time, and they now know that they can write their holiday wishes to make sure the right person knows! Christmas cards to send to classmates or family members are also fun to make in the Writing Center. Provide card stock or heavy paper and envelopes for students to use.

JANUARY

In many parts of the country, January is a cold and snowy month, while in other parts of the country, it is mild or warm and sunny. Regardless of the weather outside, students can learn about snow, cold weather, and "winter" activities by reading books. Reading is a way to "see" children sliding down snow-covered hills, children making a snowman with family or friends, people sliding or gliding on ice, and to "see how" and "why" people of all ages bundle up to keep warm when the temperature drops. Students can also learn how animals and birds survive these cold winter days.

THE OPENING

The opening continues with the calendar—it is not only a new month but a "new" year, too. Children are familiar with the days of the week and the date, but they have a new concept to work on—the order of the months, beginning with January. *Chicken Soup with Rice* by Maurice Sendak (Harper & Row, 1962) is a good book to read to the class at this time. Not only does it take students through the year month by month, it does it in rhyme. Talk about the months and how each one is a little different from the others. Talk about the rhymes in the book as well. Can most of your kindergarten students hear the rhymes now? Read *Chicken Soup With Rice* twice; it is mighty nice!

January is an interesting month to watch the thermometer and see how often it goes below freezing in your section of the country. The opening is a good time to graph the temperature each day, as well as talk about types of weather: sunny, cloudy, windy, rainy, or snowy. The morning message may be weather-related or tell about any special plans for the day.

> Dear Class,
>
> Yesterday, we made a snowman.
>
> Today, we will bring him inside.
>
> What will happen to him?
>
> Watch and see!
>
> Love,
>
> Miss Williams

Talk as you write, thinking aloud about what you are writing and why. Stretch out the big words like *yesterday* and *happen* so the children can see how adults react to words about which they are unsure. Let the students spell many of the words for you—especially the high-frequency words they know: *we*, *to*, *will*, *a*, *and*, *see*, etc.

The routine of the opening does not change, but the subjects and the weather do! There is a lot for five-year-olds to think about, talk about, and learn about during the opening. **As the year progresses, the amount of learning expected of these students grows as their knowledge of the world and words grows.**

READING ALOUD TO CHILDREN

Favorite winter stories to read in January:

Busy Year, A by Leo Lionni (Scholastic, Inc., 1992).

Chicken Soup with Rice by Maurice Sendak (Harper & Row, 1962).

Child's Year, A by Joan Walsh Anglund (Little Golden Books, 1992).

First Snow by Emily Arnold McCully (Harper Trophy, 1985).

Hello, Snow! by Wendy Cheyette Lewison (Grosset & Dunlap, 1994).

Katy and the Big Snow by Virginia Lee Burton (Scholastic, Inc., 1971).

Mike Mulligan and the Steam Shovel by Virginia Lee Burton (Houghton Mifflin, 1977).

Mitten, The retold by Jan Brett (G. P. Putnam's Sons, 1989).

Mitten, The by Krystyna Stasiak (Houghton Mifflin, 1991).

Old Man's Mitten: A Ukrainian Tale, The retold by Yevonne Pollock (Mondo, 1994).

100th Day of School, The by Angela Shelf Medevas (Scholastic, Inc., 1996).

Owl Moon by Jane Yolen (Putnam & Grosset Group, 1987).

Polar Bear, Polar Bear, What Do You Hear? by Bill Martin, Jr. (Henry Holt & Co., 1991).

Snowy Day, The by Ezra Jack Keats (Puffin Books, 1976).

When It Snows by JoAnne Nelson (Modern Curriculum Press, 1992).

Winter: Discovering the Season by Louis Sentry (Troll Associates, 1983).

READING AND WRITING WITH CHILDREN— Shared Reading of Predictable Books Followed by Writing a Predictable Chart

Snow on Snow on Snow by Cheryl Chapman (Dial Books, 1994) is a predictable book that comes in both little and big sizes. It is the story of a boy and his dog, Clancy, going out in the snow one day to play. It is a perfect day for sledding with friends. The dog enjoys the ride down the hill as much as the boy does, but when they spin out at the end, the dog disappears in the snow. Tears freeze on the boy's face until he finally hears a woof—and finds his dog below the snow drifts.

Read and Reread the Book

Read the book to the children, displaying the illustrations and inviting children's reactions. Even if you live in an area that does not receive snow, children like to hear stories about this mysterious white stuff!

The repetition in this story is noticeable from the start: "Once upon a winter's day I woke up under blankets under blankets under blankets. At breakfast mama filled up my plate with food next to food next to food. I pulled on clothes over clothes over clothes. We stepped out of the door into snow on snow on snow."

Almost every sentence includes a phrase that is said three times. On the second reading of the story, have the children help you find these repeated phrases. Then, read the story again and let the children chime in and share the reading.

Act It Out

Reread the story again, having all the children act out the story as you read it—pretending to get up and get ready, go outside to play, lose their dog in the snow (How do they feel? How do they show that they are sad?), and then find their dog. (How do they feel now? How do they look and act?)

What Do You Notice?

Write 3-5 sentences from the book on chart paper or on sentence strips that you place in your pocket chart. Once again, ask your students what they notice about the sentences you have written. Do they notice that some words look alike and are spelled alike? Can they find several words that are alike in each sentence? What else do they notice? The students can show you what they know about letters, sounds, words, and sentences when you ask this question.

Make a Predictable Chart

Following any story, a predictable chart can be written with the students. "If it Snowed" could be the title of this chart. Students can tell the class what they would like to do in the snow following the predictable pattern of "I would ...." (Examples: "I would make a snowman." or "I would make snow angels.") Remember to include the child's name in parentheses at the end of his or her sentence.

Sentence Builders

The following day, each child could "touch read" his or her sentence. Next, the students will become sentence builders. Choose three or four sentences from the chart, write them on sentence strips, and cut them apart. Beginning with the first sentence, select the same number of students as there are words in the sentence. Remember to select the student whose sentence you are using. Give each of the selected children a different word. Let the student who told you the sentence be his or her own name. Have the children come to the front of the room with their words and see if they can build the sentence by getting in the right order. Being the name portion of the sentence is always the easiest task. All children can read their own names and know where to stand—at the end!

Making a Class Book

Finally, each child will get his or her own sentence. Decide whether to give the children their sentences already cut into words, as you have done in the past, or to let them cut apart their own sentence word by word. The children will then paste these cutup sentences on drawing paper and illustrate them. When each child has completed a page, put all the pages together and bind them into a book. Now you have a winter book for your students to enjoy in the Reading Center.

READING ALOUD TO CHILDREN AND SHARED WRITING WITH CHILDREN

Another favorite book to read to kindergarten children in the winter is the Ukrainian folktale *The Mitten* adapted by Jan Brett (G. P. Putnam's Sons, 1989). There are several other versions of this tale. In *The Mitten*, a boy named Nicki wants his grandmother, Baba, to knit him a pair of mittens as white as snow. She worries that the new mittens will be easy to lose in the snow. Sure enough, while playing outdoors, Nicki loses one of his snow-white mittens. He cannot find it in the snow, but the woodland animals do. It becomes the crowded home for a mole, a rabbit, a hedgehog, an owl, a badger, a fox, a bear, and even a tiny mouse! When the mouse tickles the bear's nose, the bear sneezes, scattering the animals and sending the mitten up in the air where Nicki catches it. Baba is happy to see Nicki safe and sound at home with both his mittens.

Read and Discuss the Story/ Shared Reading

You may want to read the story every day— but you may want to read different versions. First, read and talk about the story, discussing both the winter scenery and the animals in the story. Are they familiar animals? Local animals? Big or small? Could they fit in the mitten? Read the story again and list the animals you meet, in the correct order, on a piece of chart paper or on the board. The next day, read another version of the story and discuss it. How is it the same or different? Reread the story and make another list of animals on the same piece of chart paper or next to the first list of animals on the board. Repeat this procedure for any other versions of the book you have, including the big book version. Compare all the versions. Let the children join you for shared reading of this story, especially the predictable versions.

Shared Writing

Finally, take another piece of chart paper and have the students write the story with you in a shared writing format. You lead the talk and let the students give you sentences about the story and what happened to the mitten. The story should now be predictable.

- The grandmother makes a pair of mittens for the boy. (Do they have to be white?)

- The boy goes outside and drops one mitten.

- Who comes along and finds the mitten? You will have to decide which animals you want in your version.

- How does the story end? Since there are several endings, you will need to decide if the class wants the mitten to end up whole or in pieces.

- Is this story real or make-believe? Could each of those animals end up inside a mitten?

As you write the chart, talk about what you are writing and why. Ask your students for help with both the composition and the spelling, so they learn how to think while writing.

Here is a sample story written by the teacher with a kindergarten class.

The Mitten

A boy wanted a pair of mittens.

His Grandma made him some new mittens.

He went out to play in the snow.

He lost a mitten.

A rabbit went in the mitten.

An owl went in the mitten.

A frog went in the mitten.

A fox went in the mitten.

A bear went in the mitten.

A mouse went in the mitten.

The bear sneezed, and out came the animals.

The boy was happy, because he found his mitten.

Making Their Own Book

Write the first sentence from the class's version of the story on a piece of paper, draw a box around each word, then duplicate this sentence for all your students. Have the children cut the words apart and paste the words back together in the correct order on a piece of construction paper. Some teachers cut the construction paper in the shape of a mitten! Let your kindergarten students illustrate the sentence. This will be page one of each child's book. Follow the same procedure for pages two through twelve on the days that follow.

When all pages of the book are complete, make a cover for each child's book and staple the cover and pages together. Write the name of the book and the student's name on the cover. Students can then take their own version of *The Mitten* home to "read" to their family and friends. It is interesting to see how many students can really read their version and how many are pretend reading at this time in kindergarten.

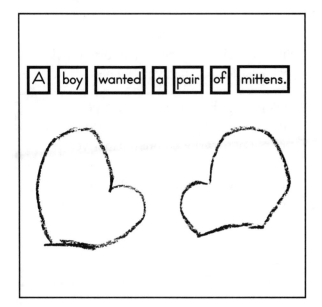

WRITING BY CHILDREN— Journal Writing

The new year is a good time to let your kindergarten students begin writing their own journal entries. Your students have been in kindergarten for almost half of the school year, and they have watched you write on numerous occasions. You have modeled journal writing for your students at the end of each day; you have written with your students as you made predictable charts; and you have also done some shared writing together with your kindergarten class. Most of your students are now ready to begin writing on their own.

Some kindergarten teachers use sheets of plain paper and a book binder to make journals for their students to use during the remainder of the year. Other kindergarten teachers staple together several sheets of paper each month so that the students start with "January Journals" and then have a new journal each month in which to write. Decide which format will work best for you and your students.

It is usually best to use plain paper for student journals because some students are not ready to write on lined paper yet. If you have a multilevel class (and most kindergarten teachers do!) then some children are ready to "drite" (draw and write), while others are ready for words or a sentence or two. The first day you ask students to write in their journals, it is a good idea to do a lesson reminding them about the ways people write.

Tell your kindergarten class that some people use pictures when they write. Draw a smiling face on the board to illustrate this.

"When you see this face, you know that someone is happy or likes what they are doing. If you drew a smiling face and a piece of pizza, what would this person be saying?"

"Yes, they are probably writing that they like pizza!"

Next, make some wavy lines (**scribble**).

"Some people pretend to write when they do not know how to write or do not know which letters to make. When you write in your journals, it is all right to pretend to write."

Then, write a few words that the students might know. (Example: cat, love, Miss Williams)

cat   love

Miss Williams

"Some people use words that they know to write a message. You know that this says cat, and this says love, and this is my name, Miss Williams."

Write a few simple sentences on the board. (Examples: I love you. I love my cat.)

I love you.   I love my cat.

While you are writing say something like

"Some of you may be able to use words and sentences when writing in your journal— just like I do. Sometimes we are not sure just what letters are in the words we want to write, so we stretch the words out and listen for the sounds we hear and write the letters that make those sounds."

Stretch out some of the words you have written on the board so that your students see you write each letter as they hear the sound (l-o-v-e, c-a-t, p-i-z-z-a).

At the conclusion of your minilesson, tell the students that when they write in their journals, they can draw, write, or both.

Encouraging **invented spelling** is one of the main ways you can help children develop their understanding of how sounds make up words. **As children try to spell words, they should**

• **say the word slowly.**

• **listen to themselves saying the sounds.**

• **think about what they have learned about letters and sounds.**

Writing daily gives children an opportunity to use their knowledge of letters, sounds, and words. It is wonderful to see young children writing what they want to say, slowly saying words and listening for the letter sounds they now know.

RHYMING BOOKS

Besides encouraging children to write the sounds that they hear (**sound spelling/spelling by ear/invented spelling/temporary spelling**), there are other activities that help children develop phonemic awareness.

Continue to read books that have some rhyming words, such as *Eeny, Meeny, Miney Mouse* by Gwen Pascoe and S. Williams (Houghton Mifflin, 1996). As always, the first reading of this book is just for enjoyment. The second time you read it to the class, ask the students to listen for rhyming words as you read. Talk about the words that rhyme on each page. Let your students hear these words:

mouse/house	**moo/shoe**	**mole/whole**
mums/crumbs	**munch/lunch**	**mat/cat**

Clapping Syllables

Another activity that may help children listen to words and separate the words into the beats they hear is "clapping syllables." You can do this with the animal names in *The Mitten* story (see Shared Writing on page 47).

- Write *owl*, *rabbit*, *frog*, *fox*, *raccoon*, and *bear* on index cards for your pocket chart or on the chalkboard.

- Tell the children you are going to say the names of the animals and they should listen for the beats they hear.

- Ask the children to clap to show how many beats each word has.

- Say each word one at a time (owl/rabbit/ frog/fox/raccoon/bear).

- Help the children decide that owl is a one-clap, one-beat word, and that rabbit takes two claps and is a two-beat word.

Once you have said all six words, do this exercise again, looking at the words as you clap the beats. **Explain that if a word has more claps it probably takes more letters to write.** How many claps for the word *animal*?

CENTERS

Reading Center

The Reading Center is filling up with books the children have heard in class and can read and pretend read. The students can also read many of the class books they helped to make. It is now time to add books with snow pictures in them to your Reading Center. It is also a wonderful time to read and discuss snowmen, sleds, skates, and snowplows.

Writing Center

The Writing Center has new words for a January Pictionary posted in the same familiar spot. There are also pieces of paper the children can use as stationery and decorate with snowmen and snowscenes. If you have a computer in your classroom, now is the time to talk about how students can "write" on computers. (Now would be a good time to ask parents to donate "old" computers to your classroom.) A computer can make writing much easier for those students for whom handwriting is difficult.

ASSESSING PROGRESS

Assessment is an ongoing process for experienced kindergarten teachers who have become good "kid watchers."

- As the children respond to various activities, teachers notice who can do what. Write down what you notice and you will have anecdotal records!

- Samples—particularly writing samples—are also informative. By comparing early and later samples of a student's work, growth can be determined and validated.

At the midpoint of the kindergarten year, most teachers want to do some individual assessment with their children. What you assess and how you do it should mirror your instruction. Some suggested tasks which will help you assess the concepts on which you have been concentrating are included in this chapter. Some children will be able to complete all these tasks successfully. Hopefully, every child will be able to do at least some of the tasks. Before you begin your assessment of the students, make sure that you have all the necessary materials. Then, decide when you will do the assessment and how many children you will assess each day. **Assessment should not take too long; try to finish your entire class in a week, if possible. "Center" time is usually a good time to do the individual assessment.**

Here are some things you should assess at the halfway point in kindergarten:

Assessing Words

Children who are progressing should have learned some of the words used in daily activities, including the names of their classmates and words used in the opening. It is not expected that they will have learned **all** the names or opening words. To assess their word learning, write the first names of the children in your class on index cards. Put them in the pocket chart or spread them out on the table in front of you. Ask each child to choose three to five of the name cards, and read them aloud to you, one card at a time. **Children who can read three to five names at this point in kindergarten are making progress with word learning.**

Do a similar activity with words used in the opening. Write some words you use each day during the opening, including **the days of the week and weather words.** Ask each child to read the names of three days of the week and three weather words.

Assessing Letter Names

You have been talking about letters and letter names during the opening, when working with children's names, when writing, when reading big books, and when asking, "What do you notice?" **It is now time to see if the children recognize some letter names.** It is not necessary for children to know all 52 upper- and lowercase letters, but they should have learned some of them. Write six non-confusing capital letters (**A**, **D**, **B**, **M**, **S**, and **R**) and six small letters (**o**, **i**, **e**, **c**, **t**, and **n**) separately on index cards or duplicate page 56. **Ask each child to pick up and name as many of the letters as they can.**

Assessing Phonemic Awareness

You have been clapping the syllables (beats) in the children's names and working with the concept of rhyme. Find out if the children are progressing in these two important areas of phonemic awareness.

Choose several of the children's names, each with a different number of syllables. Ask each child individually to say the name after you and clap the beats. For example, if you said *Jasmine*, the student would repeat the name and clap twice. The child would also clap twice for the name *Ryan*. For a name like *Paul*, the child would clap only once.

To assess rhyme, collect six pictures of common objects which have rhyming names or duplicate page 55.

bike	bed
cat	cake
van	bus

Name the six pictures with the child, and then have the child name them all for you. Next, tell the child that you are going to say a name and he or she is to repeat the name and find a picture that rhymes with it. Do one together as an example:

> "The first name is *Ted*. Say *Ted* and then the names of the pictures. Show me which picture rhymes with *Ted*."

Help the child to realize that *Ted* and *bed* rhyme. Have the child say *"Ted-bed"* several times and remove the bed picture. Now there are five pictures left. **Name each of the five pictures and have the child repeat the names and find the picture that rhymes with each of the following names:**

Mike	Pat	Jake
Dan	Gus	

Assessing Print Concepts

Reading requires some particular ways of moving your eyes and an understanding of jargon such as **word**, **letter**, and so on. Often, children who do not come from literacy-rich homes are confused by this jargon. Although all children speak in words, they do not know words exist as separate entities until they start reading and writing at school. **To many children, letters are what you get in the mailbox; sounds are horns, bells, and slamming doors; and a sentence is what a person has to serve if he gets caught committing a crime!** These children may be unable to follow your "simple" instructions because you are using words which, for them, either have no meaning or an entirely different meaning. All year, you have helped children develop the concepts and jargon of print that they need to progress in reading. Now it is time to assess how their print concepts are developing.

For this assessment, use a predictable book used for shared reading or one of the class big books you created from a predictable chart. **First, ask the student to show you the front of the book. Turn to the first page and ask the child to point to where they would start to read and to point to words for you to read. Notice if the student is pointing to just one word and making the correct return sweep.**

Next, ask the child to **point to just one word, anywhere on the page.** Then, **have the child point to the first word on the page, and then the last word on the page.** Ask the child to **point to just one letter, anywhere on the page.** Then, **pick a word from the page and ask the student to point to the first letter in the word and the last letter in the word.**

Concepts of Print Checklist

- Finds the front of a book

- Starts on left side of the page

- Goes left to right across the page

- Makes return sweep to next line

- Matches words by pointing to each word as he or she reads it

- Can point to just one word

- Can point to the first word and the last word

- Can point to just one letter

- Can point to the first letter and the last letter of a word

Using Assessment Results

You can create your own assessment record sheet for each student or use the one on page 54 to write down the results of your assessment. Analyze the progress each child is making. Make a list of the names of children who do not seem to be progressing as quickly as they should on a class summary sheet. Put this sheet in a place where you will see it often and use it as a reminder of the students on whom to focus during your activities for the upcoming month. While reading big books or predictable charts, ask the children who still cannot track print to be your "pointers" during the activity. Help these students to show just one word, the last word in the sentence, and so on. Likewise, during the morning message and other activities with words, move the children who need work with word learning and letter name knowledge closer to you and call on them more often. Provide individual coaching and "nudges" to these children as you work with the group. Ask the children whose syllable-clapping and rhyming responses indicate difficulty in developing phonemic awareness to lead rhyming and clapping activities with you. Many teachers also work individually or in a small group with children who still need additional time and practice by rereading big books or charts and by focusing on these concepts, especially during center time. At the end of next month, reassess the students about whose progress you are concerned, concentrating on the concepts with which the students had problems.

Student Name _____	JAN.	MAR.	JUNE
Words—Can recognize			
3 names			
3 days of the week			
3 weather words			
Letter Names—Can recognize			
A D B M S R			
o i e c t n			
Phonemic Awareness			
Can clap the beats for 3 names			
Matches pictures with rhyming words			
Concepts of Print			
Finds the front of a book			
Starts on left side of the page			
Goes left to right across the page			
Makes return sweep to next line			
Matches words by pointing to each word as reading			
Can point to just one word			
Can point to the first word and the last word			
Can point to just one letter			
Can point to the first letter and the last letter of a word			

Comments

R	n
S	t
M	c
B	e
D	i
A	o

February is another cold winter month in many parts of the country. In some places there is a "winter vacation" from school so students (and teachers!) can enjoy the snow and winter activities. In other places in the country, snow may mean no school as traffic and activities come to a stop. What happens at your school depends upon the area of the country in which you live, but wherever you live, snow is fascinating to young children.

THE OPENING

The Opening continues with the same routine you established months ago. **Young children thrive on routine because they know what to do and when to do it.** Students answer questions and look at the words that have now become familiar to them—the days of the week, the names of the months, and weather words. Since these words are already familiar to the children, use them to teach more about letter/sound correspondence.

Teacher: "How do we know this word is *Wednesday*?"

Student: "It begins with a *W*."

Teacher: "How do you know that it isn't *Tuesday*?"

Student: "Because it does not have a *T* at the beginning."

Teacher: "What is the weather outside like today?"

Student: "Cold and cloudy."

Teacher: "Who can come up and show me the word *cold*?"

Student: (Points to the weather word *cold* on the bulletin board.)

Teacher: "Who can come find the word *cloudy*?"

Student: (Points to the word *cloudy* on the bulletin board.)

Teacher: "How do you know that word is *cloudy*?"

Student: "Because it begins with a *cl*. "

(If the student answers that cloudy begins with a *c*, point out that *cold* began with a *c* as well. Then say, "Listen to the word *cloudy*. (Stretch out the pronunciation of cl-o-u-d-y so that the children can hear the two sounds blended together at the beginning.) What two letters do you hear at the beginning of *cloudy*?"

If your students have been counting the days of school by bundling straws together into "tens," **it should be almost time to celebrate one hundred days of school.** (It usually happens sometime in February.) The ten "tens" now go into a bigger bundle so children can see what one hundred straws look like. Some teachers ask their students to bring in other sets of hundreds—100 pennies, 100 pieces of candy, 100 peanuts, 100 raisins, etc. and then display these in the room. **Kindergarten children have reached a milestone in "real" school: 100 days of literacy and learning!**

There is still time to read all those winter stories your students love even if you do not live where it is cold enough to snow. It is also a good time to talk about what happens to birds, animals, plants, and people in the winter.

Some teachers use penguins, presidents, or hibernation as February themes. As Valentine's Day approaches, "love" is also a wonderful theme to use, and kindergarten children enjoy making hearts and valentines and reading and writing about love. Students talk about the people they love and the things they love to do. Some classes even make cookies and decorate them with pink or red frosting for a Valentine's Day party.

Morning Message

The opening is the time to talk about what is going to happen each day. Write a morning message for your children telling them about the day's events. Although the concept of the morning message is not "new" any longer, the content of each message is new and the children are excited about reading the message each day. When you write "Dear Class," it is now familiar to the students. From repetition, they know that the morning message starts this way and so does a letter or note to a friend or relative.

Dear Class,

Today, we are going to make valentines.

We will write "I love you" inside.

               Love,

               Miss Williams

Kindergarten students know how to read and write the word "love" because you have signed your morning message this way every-day. As you write your morning message, let the students spell out the word love ("l-o-v-e") for you. The body of the message is always a puzzle to them, but students will look for words they know and letters and sounds they can figure out until some (with a little help from you) have decoded today's event.

Tongue Twisters

Tongue twisters help develop phonemic awareness. As children listen for beginning sounds that are alike their brains become pattern detectors. As they look at the tongue twister, they see the same beginning letter in print. Tongue twisters help link phonemic awareness (oral) and phonics (visual).

The children have learned a lot about letters and sounds, so begin placing a new and different tongue twister on the chalkboard, bulletin board, or in the pocket chart each day during the opening.

- Point to the words as you read the tongue twister to the class. "Noisy Nora nibbles on nutritious nuts."

- Ask the class which words begin alike and what letter is at the beginning of those words.

- Ask the students to listen again as you read the tongue twister.

- See if the students know any other words that begin with the same "n" sound. Almost every child will contribute an "n" word!

"nice"	"nickel"	"nose"
"NO"	"napkin"	"noodles"
"nine"	"nest"	"night"
"Nintendo"	"Nikki"	"November"

Here are some tongue twisters you may want to use with your class:

Aunt Annie always ate apples alone.

Boo Boo Bear has a brown bow and a blue balloon.

Carol's cat carries carrots in a cart.

David's dog digs deep down in the dirt.

Eddie the elephant eats every egg.

Felicia and Freddy fight for fast food on Friday.

Gus the groundhog gathered goodies from Gail's garden.

Happy Henry happily hugged Hilda and Hank.

Iggy Inchworm inches into an igloo.

Jolly Jimmy jumps for joy in January.

Katy and Kevin Kangaroo keep flying kites.

Little Lucy likes lots of lollipops to lick.

Miss Mouse munches on marvelous marsh-mallows.

Noisy Nora nibbles on nutritious nuts.

Ollie Octopus eats okra, onions, and oranges.

Pretty Peggy plants pumpkins in a path.

Ricky Rabbit gives Ruthy Raccoon red roses.

Silly Sally sings songs about her senses.

Tom Turkey took ten turtles to town.

The unusual unicorn sat under an umbrella.

Vera has violets, vegetables, a vacuum, and a van.

Willy the wild wolf went west for the winter.

Extra! Extra! Read all about **Xx** in fox, six, and x-ray.

Yolanda yelled, "Yikes, get that yak out of my yard!"

A zany zebra zipped a zillion zippers.

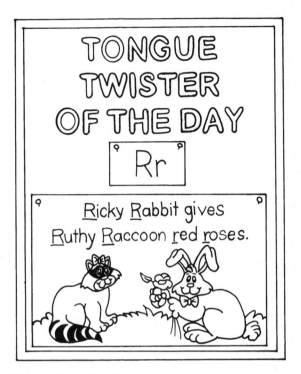

The Alphabet

This month, read alphabet books to your students as you focus more on letters and sounds. "The Alphabet Song" has been sung by generations of children. Students enjoy the song, and it seems to give them a sense of all of the letters and a framework in which to put new letters as they learn them. Many children come to school already able to sing "The Alphabet Song." Let these children teach the song to everyone else in the class. Once all the children in the class can sing the song, you may want to point to alphabet cards (usually placed above the chalkboard) while the students sing.

Children enjoy "being the alphabet" as they line up to go somewhere. Pass out some laminated alphabet cards—one to each child, leftovers to the teacher—and let the children sing the song slowly as they line up. Be sure to hand out the cards randomly so that no one gets to be the A and lead the line or has to be the Z and bring up the rear every day!

READING ALOUD TO CHILDREN— Alphabet books

There are many wonderful alphabet books to read and enjoy with your students. Many of these books fit into your themes or units. **Research shows that simple books with a few words on a page and pictures that most children recognize are the most helpful in building a child's letter-sound and letter-name knowledge.** Once a book has been read and reread several times, children will enjoy reading it for themselves when they go to the Reading Center. **It is very important that children have time to read books of their own choosing each day.** Simple alphabet books which have been read together as a class are items that students can read on their own.

Here are some alphabet books that meet the "not too many words, familiar pictures, and kids love to read them" criteria:

A, My Name is Alice by Jane Bayer (Dial Books, 1984).

A You're Adorable by Buddy Kaye et al. (Candlewick Press, 1994).

Accidental Zucchini: An Unexpected Alphabet by Max Grover (Harcourt Brace, 1993).

All Aboard ABC by Doug Magee and Robert Newman (Philomel, 1993).

Alphabet City by Stephen T. Johnson (Viking Press, 1995).

Alphabet Tale, The by Jan Garten (Random House, 1964).

Alphabetics by Suse MacDonald (Bradbury Press, 1986).

Animal ABCs by Susan Hood (Troll Assoc., 1995).

By the Sea: An Alphabet Book by Ann Blades (Kids Can Press, 1985).

Dr. Seuss's ABC by Theodore Seuss Geisel (Random House, 1963).

Eating the Alphabet: Fruits and Vegetables from A to Z by Lois Ehlert (Harcourt Brace, 1989).

From Acorn to Zoo and Everything in Between in Alphabetical Order by Satoshi Kitamura (Farrar, Straus, and Giroux, 1992).

It Begins with an A by Stephanie Calmenson (Hyperion, 1993).

K is for Kiss Goodnight: A Bedtime Alphabet by Jill Sardegan (Doubleday, 1994).

NBA Action from A to Z by James Preller (Scholastic, Inc., 1997).

On Market Street by Arnold Lobel (Greenwillow Books, 1981).

Sleepy ABC by Margaret Wise Brown (HarperCollins, 1994).

Where Is Everybody? by Eve Merrimam (Simon & Schuster, 1989; Big Book by Scott Foresman, 1996).

READING WITH CHILDREN—
Shared Reading With Predictable Big Books

There are many big books that are really alphabet books, including Big Book Dictionaries. Three Big Book Dictionaries that are wonderful to use in kindergarten are *My Big Dictionary* (Houghton Mifflin, 1994), *From Acorn to Zoo and Everything in Between in Alphabetical Order* (previously cited), and *My Picture Dictionary* edited by D. Snowball and R. Greene (Mondo, 1994). Use these dictionaries to talk about letters, sounds, and words during the opening or tongue twisters.

My Big Dictionary contains a picture page for each letter of the alphabet. Children can have fun finding the words in the picture that begin with that particular letter.

From Acorn to Zoo and Everything in Between in Alphabetical Order can be used for shared reading with your students. On each page in the book is a letter and 15-20 words that begin with that letter. At the bottom of every page is a question, such as "What is the armadillo balancing on his nose?" The answer to the question can be found in the list of "a" words—apple, apricot, almond, and acorn. The second time you read it, point to the pictures and have the students "read the pictures" and answer the question at the bottom of each page.

By looking at the picture on the page, they can find the answer to each question. Kindergarten students like to share the "work" of finding the answer to the question as they look at the pictures and think of words that match the print (same letter, same sound, same size, etc.).

My Picture Dictionary has several special features. Each page includes simple pictures and print for the letter. Down the side of the page, the entire alphabet is listed with a character to indicate the letter for the words on that page. It is available in big book for whole class modeling, as well as hard and soft cover small book formats.

Your kindergarten students will enjoy "reading" these dictionaries in the Reading Center when you finish your class activities. Pairs of students can read the dictionaries, with one student being the "teacher" and asking questions, and the other being the "student" and answering the questions. The pictures will help those who cannot read all the words.

After reading several ABC books, it is fun for the children to make their own ABC books. One way to do this is to have each child make a page for his or her book every time you begin a new tongue twister and letter sound. This is another project that will not be completed within a month's time because there are twenty-six pages to make plus the book cover.

ABC and You by Eugenie Fernandes (Houghton Mifflin, 1996) is another alphabet big book you can read to the class. The children find it easy to share the reading once they know that it starts with Amazing Amanda and ends with Zippy Zack. It's fun to make your own "ABC and You" predictable chart. Whose name begins with A? B? C? Your predictable chart can begin with Amazing Allie or Adorable Adam and continue with Jumping Jasmine and Marvelous Mike until you get to the end of your class with Wonderful William or Zany Zack. This will help the children to focus on their names and to think of other words that begin with the same letters and sounds. Some letters will have more than one name; other letters will have no one to represent them unless you decide to make up a person's name for the missing letters.

PREDICTABLE CHARTS

There are many types of ABC books from which you can make predictable charts with your class. After reading an alphabet book, begin a predictable chart by writing the first sentence:

A is for apple. (Miss Williams)

The children know what letter comes next, and they raise their hands because they are ready to contribute.

A is for apple. (Miss Williams)
B is for bee. (Suzanne)
C is for cat. (Jasmine)
D is for dog. (Ryan)
E is for elephant. (Michelle)
F is for fish. (Paul)
G is for goat. (Joyce)
H is for hat. (Nikki)
I is for ice cream. (Rayshaun)
J is for jam. (Emily)
K is for kids. (Mitchell)
L is for LOVE. (Olivia)
M is for monkey. (Adam)
N is for nuts. (Refugio)
O is for orange. (William)
P is for pie. (Erica)
Q is for quiet. (Mike)
R is for rope. (Jacob)
S is for snake! (Jimmy)
T is for towels. (Julie)
U is for umbrella. (Tiara)
V is for valentine. (Marie)
W is for window. (Pat)
X is for x-ray.
Y is for yellow.
Z is for zoo.

Sometimes the class is not large enough to have a student response for every letter, so for the last few letters the teacher and class may need to think of some sentences together. Rereading this chart is fun because the children see their names in print and can read their own sentence. As they reread the chart, have each child "touch read" his or her sentence—touching each word as he or she reads it. This is a way you can see if each child is tracking print and developing voice-to-print match. The children should also know where their first name falls in ABC order.

Sentence Builders

On the following day, the children can read their sentences and become sentence builders. Choose four or five sentences from the chart, write them on sentence strips, cut them apart into words, and give each word in the sentence to a different child. Beginning with the first sentence, have the children come to the front of the class with their words and "build the sentence" by getting in the right order.

The first five children, including Suzanne (whose sentence the students are building), come to the front of the class and build the sentence, "B is for bee. (Suzanne)" With the rest of the class, read and "check" the sentence. The next group of sentence builders comes to the front and follows the same procedure.

Making a Class ABC Book

After four or five sentences have been built, it is time for each child to cut apart the words in his or her sentence and put them back in the right order. Earlier, you cut apart the sentences for your students. Now that the students understand that sentences are made up of words, kindergartners are ready to do this task by themselves. If you have a few students who have trouble with this task, you can use their sentences to demonstrate or you can cut the sentences apart for them. Some students will need more help than others.

Each student then rearranges the words of his or her cutup sentence on a large piece of drawing paper to make it look just as it does on the predictable chart. Some kindergarten students have to look at the chart to be sure they are right. Other students can read all the words and need no help with this task. After

you check to see that the words are in the right order, the students can paste their sentences down on the bottom of their papers. Finally, each student draws a picture to illustrate his or her sentence. Suzanne takes crayons and draws a big yellow and black bee—including the stinger. She was stung by bees twice last summer, and she knows what bees look like! Ryan draws his dog, a dalmatian with big black spots. Olivia draws a fancy red heart for LOVE. After illustrating their sentences, the children are ready to line up in ABC order and put the class book together.

Miss Williams begins with her "A" page—the one she used to demonstrate writing a sentence on the predictable chart, cutting the sentence apart, and then pasting and illustrating it. Suzanne knows that "B" is next, so she brings her sentence to the front of the room. Jasmine follows with her cat picture for "C." Ryan knows that his "dog" is after the "cat." Michelle is next, and she's proud that she has the biggest picture and the biggest word—elephant. She helps Paul to find his place with his "fish" picture. The students have fun getting everyone's pictures in the right place, using the predictable chart to check themselves. When the pages are in alphabetical order, put a piece of heavy colored construction paper on each side of the pages for the front and back cover. Bind the covers and pages together with the school's book binder (if one is available) or staple them together. Then, add this class-made big book to the Reading Center. With this big book, your students will have yet another opportunity to work with letters, sounds, familiar words, and names.

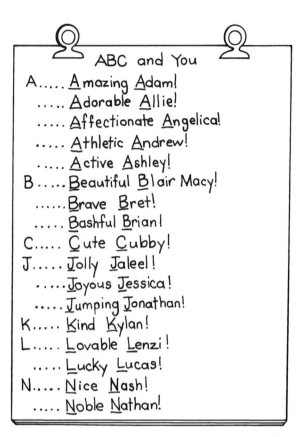

ABC and You

A..... Amazing Adam!
..... Adorable Allie!
..... Affectionate Angelica!
..... Athletic Andrew!
..... Active Ashley!
B..... Beautiful Blair Macy!
..... Brave Bret!
..... Bashful Brian!
C..... Cute Cubby!
J..... Jolly Jaleel!
..... Joyous Jessica!
..... Jumping Jonathan!
K..... Kind Kylan!
L..... Lovable Lenzi!
..... Lucky Lucas!
N..... Nice Nash!
..... Noble Nathan!

There are other ABC books you can make. Once you have read and reread the book *ABC and You*, do shared writing with your class using students' names. Write "ABC and You" on the top of a large piece of chart paper. Ask the students to decide whose name begins with A and write it down, along with a descriptive adjective that begins with the same letter (Amazing Adam, Adorable Allie). Let the children decide whose sentence will be next, depending on the student's first name and where it falls in alphabetical order.

After the chart is completed, you can write each child's sentence on a sentence strip. Or, you may want your students to copy their sentences on sentence strips or large pieces of paper. As you reread the predictable chart, have the children get in line with their sentences in alphabetical order. The third reading may be done by the children who are lined up in ABC order by their first names. If you have Michelle, Mike, and Mitchell, you will have to help them get in the right places. You do not need to teach ABC order by second and third letters, but you can mention it as you put Michelle in front of Mike, and Mike in front of Mitchell. There may be one or two students who pick up on what you are doing and why, making this a multilevel activity. Once again, the students draw pictures to illustrate their sentences and put the drawings together in alphabetical order to make a class book. Other ideas for class alphabet books include animal alphabets (especially if your theme is animals) or classroom alphabet books (finding objects in the classroom that begin with the letters of the alphabet).

DEVELOPING PHONEMIC AWARENESS— Rhyming Books

A wonderful winter book to read is *When It Snows* by JoAnne Nelson (previously cited). This book is written in rhyming questions.

  "Will you dance with your own shadow as it falls across the snow, and wave your arms and fingers so your shadow seems to grow?"

The pictures and the questions are fun to talk about and think about with any kindergarten class.

Valentine's Day by Miriam Nerlove (Albert Whitman, 1992) is another rhyming book which contains a brief history of Valentine's Day, followed by a little girl's account of this celebration at home and at school. Many kindergarten teachers read this book, or other books that are similar to it, to their class. Do not miss the opportunity to discuss the rhyming words as well as the holiday.

Many alphabet books are written in rhyme. *It Begins with an A* written by Stephanie Calmenson (previously cited) is one example. During the first reading of this book, kindergarten children usually like to answer the question, "What is it?" for each of the letters of the alphabet. Read the book a second time and talk about the rhyming words!

Do not forget Dr. Seuss's books! Although we have mentioned them before, his books are a rich source of rhyming words and wonderful examples of playing with words. *Cat in the Hat* by Dr. Seuss (Random House, 1966) is a popular book among emerging readers. Read this book to your class; those students who have heard it before enjoy it just as much as those students who have never before heard it. Read it a second time and listen for the rhyming pairs of words, including *cat* and *hat* from the title. This book has easy spelling patterns for young children to see and with which to experiment. There are a lot of words kindergartners know that rhyme with *cat* and *hat*, and it is fun to see how many words they can find.

Making Words

You can work on phonemic awareness with your students by doing a "making words" activity which is appropriate for kindergarten. Paste large cut out black letters on sheets of white construction paper, then laminate the sheets. (This will make saving and reusing the letters time after time possible.) Punch holes at the top on each side of the sheet of paper, and tie lengths of yarn through the holes. The yarn should be long enough to tie around your students' necks. Or, you may wish to purchase yellow vinyl "letter vests" available from some school supply catalogs. These vests usually have a lower case letter printed on one side and the corresponding capital letter printed on the reverse side. Choose two students to become the *at* rhyme or spelling pattern (one for the *a* card/vest and one for the *t* card/vest). The other children become the letters *b, c, h, f, m, p, s,* and *r.* Let the students who spell *c-a-t* stand in front of the classroom. Say the letters *c-a-t* and then say the word "cat." Take away the *c* by having the child who is the *c* sit down or move off to the side. Read aloud what is left of the original word—"at." Then, have the other letters (students) come up and stand with "at." Let the students notice that it is important that they stand in front of "at." See who can read the new words as the children who are holding letter cards or wearing letter vests come to the front and join "at" (*mat, pat,* etc.). This manipulation of letters and sounds to make new words is an important part of learning to read.

WRITING BY CHILDREN— Self-Selected WritingTopics

In kindergarten classes where teachers have been writing a morning message, a journal entry, and predictable charts with their students, you find students who are writing and enjoying it. Many students have been writing "on their own" in their journals and at the Writing Center. **Now it is time to give all students a chance to self-select their own writing topics. Research tells us that children write best when they write about things they know.**

Most teachers try to give students topics about which all students have prior knowledge—the themes they are studying, the coming holidays, things that are happening at school, etc. During journal writing time, most children begin to write stories in their journals about the things they find interesting: the basketball game they watched last night, their family's trip to the beach, their pet, etc. **The topics students pick should not be limited to just your ideas. If you have not already done so, give your students permission to write about topics they know. Young children expand and "piggyback" on their peers' topics and ideas.**

Most children write "all about" stories—all about their dog or cat, all about their family, or all they know about basketball. Once in a while, you may have a student who attempts to write fiction, usually beginning his or her story with the words "Once upon a time...." In kindergarten, fiction is not as familiar as the "all about" stories and should be recognized for the writing feat that it is.

If you have been writing **for** and **with** your students daily, then you may notice that the students are really beginning to express themselves in writing.

For example, Seth writes about his favorite college basketball team.

3-11   Seth

i lik Wat Fos Wat Fos is nab 1.

i lik wchen the bskti bol gam.

Wat Fos ol mst lost.

it wzs fnny wchen the bskti bol gam.

i pugl for Wat Fos.

Go WFU!!!

Seth

I like Wake Forest. Wake Forest is number 1.

I like watching the basketball game.

Wake Forest almost lost.

It was funny watching the basketball game.

I pulled for Wake Forest.

Go WFU!!!

Rebecca writes about a day in her kindergarten class.

Rebecca   February-21

Daer Boys and Gruls.

I am in Mrs.Wares Class.

We Writ Storys in The Lab.

We are Good in School.

We Have Cintres Win We Get To School.

We Wolket To The Post Ofice We Got Stamps At The Post Office.

We Go On Filltrips.

We Have Lunch At 11:45.

Aftre The Silent Of Momit Bell Rings We Go To The Grop.

We Work At Cintres.

We Work Hard At Cintres.

We Do The Calindr and Wethr in The Mornin.

Most Of Us Do Ore Best Work.

We Have Snak Aftre We Come From The Lab.

Aftre Snak Mrs. Ruminsky Comes .She Hlops The Childrin She Hlops The Childrin Lron Ther Numbrs and Ther Leders.

I Rot This NOt all By My Self.

Rebecca

Dear Boys and Girls.

I am in Mrs. Ware's class.

We write stories in the lab.

We are good in school.

We have centers when we get to school.

We walked to the Post Office. We got stamps at the Post Office.

We go on fieldtrips.

We have lunch at 11:45.

After the Moment of Silence bell rings we go to the group.

We work at centers.

We work hard at centers.

We do the calendar and weather in the morning.

Most of us do our best work.

We have snack after we come from the lab.

After snack Mrs. Ruminsky comes. She helps the children. She helps the children learn their numbers and their letters.

I wrote this note all by myself.

Other students write about their friends, their family, and the things they do.

> Brendan   2-28
>
> I Can pla wth mi fish
> I wnt to the moll with mi dad and
>   brothr to buy fish
> for mi aqreum

Brendan
I can play with my fish.
I went to the mall with my dad and
      brother to buy fish
for my aquarium.

> Carol   2-22
>
> My mommy thiks my daddy
>   is fat
> I lik my mommy.
> I lik my daddy.

Carol
My mommy thinks my daddy is fat.
I like my mommy.
I like my daddy.

Some kindergarten students will take a "risk" and write fiction. Do you notice the Southern accent?

> 2-27   bailey
>
> wons upon a tim a litl gol had
> a haond. tat nit the haond ran
> in to the forist. the litl gol
> cod not fiend hm. the litl gol was
> wored. the haond sol a fox. tha
> wr best frans. tha navr did bad thags to ej
> othr. tha wr bast frans for avr. the fox and
> the haond

Bailey (Southern accent and fiction)
Once upon a time a little girl had a hound. That night the hound ran into the forest. The little girl could not find him. The little girl was worried. The hound saw a fox. They were best friends. They never did bad things to each other. They were best friends forever, the fox and the hound.

Coaching Writing and Using Invented Spelling

How did these young students get so good at writing? They had teachers who modeled what writing is and how to think and write each day during the morning message and journal writing. Their teachers also took the time to coach them. Coaching means sitting down with the students and helping them to "say" what they want to write, and then helping them to listen for the words they know how to write (words they have seen in print all year), and then helping them to stretch out the words they do not know by listening for the sounds they can represent with letters. When you write a child's sentence instead of having him or her write it, you do not know what he or she actually knows about letter/sound relationships or words. When children "invent" the words they do not know, you learn about their word knowledge and how they represent sounds in the words they are writing. If kindergarten children are limited to writing only the words they can spell correctly, then they cannot write very much. If you write the words the students cannot spell on their papers, you will know nothing about what they know about the word. The only thing you know is that they could not spell the word and wanted you to write it for them. If you say, "Stretch that word out and listen for the sounds you hear" ("ear spelling" or "sound spelling"), then you have a mirror into what the children know about the word. You will learn how many phonemes the students can hear and know how to represent. Notice that Carol and Brendan do not have the word knowledge that Rebecca and Seth have—but Brendan is learning to listen for beginning and ending sounds and can even represent some vowel sounds.

After seeing the writing samples on the previous pages, some of you may be thinking, "My kindergarten kids can't write like that."

They *can* and *will* if you believe they can and continue to model and coach their developing writing skills.

For kindergarten teachers who have not read J. Richard Gentry's work on the stages of spelling (writing) development, his article in *Early Years K-8* (May 1985) titled, "You Can Analyze Developmental Spelling—And Here's How To Do It!" or his two books, *Spel. . . .is a Four Letter Word* (Heinemann Books, 1989) and *Teaching Kids to Spell* with Jean Wallace Gillet (Heinemann Books, 1992), can give you a better understanding of how young children learn to spell and write. These five spelling stages are listed on the following pages, along with samples of students' work for each of the stages.

Gentry writes that a teacher's awareness of children's developmental spelling progress enables him or her to respond intelligently when working with students. During writing time, a teacher has an opportunity to both respond to and coach the students so that they can become better writers and better spellers as they learn more about words and writing. What the teacher says and does with students daily depends upon the students with which he or she is working and what they know.

Stages of Spelling Development

Stage 1: The Precommunicative or Pre-phonemic Stage

This is the stage before children know about phonemes—letters and letter sounds. Spelling and writing at this stage contains scribbles (see Corey) or random letters (see Sarah, Tony, and Angelica).

Corey scribbles when asked to write. He has no letters or words in his writing. Often, children use wavy lines in their attempts to imitate their parents' writing.

Sarah writes with random letters, "I love my mommy and I love my sister." Notice there is no correspondence between letters and sounds in words. Sarah knows that you can use letters to represent the sounds you hear in words—she just doesn't know which ones!

Tony writes about all the things he loves, too. "I love dad. I love mom. I love basketball. I love pizza...." Tony knows that there are words in sentences. (His teacher has been writing predictable charts!) He has more word knowledge than Sarah, but like Sarah, he has not figured out which letters represent which sounds.

```
TONY 2-27
I UG p
i hr t
i fd l
i cr t
i ju k
i kt z
```

Angelica has copied the alphabet in the room, and then she writes some random letters (Ns and Os) and draws pictures. Angelica "copies." Children at this stage like to copy if they know that letters can represent sounds, but they do not know which ones.

Stage 2: The Semiphonetic Stage

The second stage can be seen when words begin to be represented by a letter or two. The letters they write are usually the first letter in a word or the first and last.

Terry represents dinosaur with a d or a dr. He listens for the sounds he hears as the word is stretched out. He writes what he hears. His story is:

Dinosaurs

Dinosaurs were born in the olden days. Dinosaurs were big. Dinosaurs had big teeth. Dinosaurs had long tails. Dinosaurs didn't have no food. (Verbally, Terry adds, "That's why we don't have dinosaurs now!")

Terry
dr
dr y b n oi dz.
d y bg.
d had bg te.
dr hd lg tailz.
dr d h no fd.

Stage 3: The Phonetic Stage

The third stage is when vowels appear—not necessarily the right vowel. The long vowels appear correctly represented first, but there is an attempt at short vowel sounds, also. Regional accents often affect how vowels are represented.

Paige writes about what she saw at the Nature Science Center. Her writing shows us that her teacher writes predictable charts, and Paige attempts to use this structure in her own writing as she tells us what she saw. (So—saw, you can hear a short o in "saw" if you say it like Paige.) Her story is:

I saw a deer. I saw ducks. I saw rabbits. I saw goats. I saw cows. I saw a snake. I saw a wild cat.

paige
i so a der.
i so duks.
i so rabbits.
i so gots.
i so cios.
i so a snak.
i so a wild cat.

Stage 4: Transitional

In this stage, the sounds are represented and the spelling is a possible English spelling. When kindergarten students are bright and allowed to write, they reach this stage quite quickly.

Christopher

I like sienc a lot.

Sienc is fun.

Sienc is neat.

My mom is goeg to git som theings for sience. I jest got a book abot sienc.

1 books name is 175 sienc etspermets.

The othr books name is hands on sienc.

I love sienc.

indins got cild a long time a go.

They livd in tpese they fitidid with

cow Boys they make thair close out

of Bofflows.

They rid horses sumtims the jump off thair horses to ciel snakes to pertek thair horses.

Thair wiepins are nivs.

Graham

Christopher

I like science a lot. Science is fun. Science is neat. My mom is going to get some things for science. I just got a book about science. One book's name is 175 Science Experiments. The other book's name is Hands On Science. I love science.

Graham

Indians got killed a long time ago. They lived in tepees. They fighted (fought) with cowboys. They made their clothes out of buffaloes. They ride horses. Sometimes, they jump off their horses to kill snakes to protect their horses. Their weapons are knives.

Step 5: Correct Spelling

We have no kindergarten writing samples for Stage 5 because very few kindergarten students can spell all words correctly, unless they limit what they want to say to known spelling words! Kindergarten students can be found going through the first four stages as they learn about words and use what they know in their daily writing.

How and When Writing is Multilevel

Writing is a multilevel activity when you let students choose their own topics and take as long as they need to write. Choosing their own topics guarantees that students are writing about something of which they have knowledge and reinforces for them the idea that what they say and write has worth. As you watch students write, you will learn that some students cannot finish a story in a day. The students at both ends of the spectrum may need more than one day to develop their stories. Some students often have more to say than one writing period allows them to write, while others write only a few words or one line during that time. To get several sentences on paper often takes some students several days. If you want writing to be a multilevel activity, you must give all students the time they need to do their best writing.

CENTERS

Reading Center

The Reading Center is now filled with many class-made books, as well as the collection of trade books and big books. Children find books they can read and other books they pretend read—but they enjoy the books regardless. The Reading Center is becoming more popular as children find out that a wonderful thing is happening to them—they are becoming **readers**! Children love to share this milestone with family members and friends. Almost every day, a few of the children will ask to take books from the Reading Center home with them so that they can share their ability to "really read" with their siblings, parents or guardians, and grandparents.

Writing Center

The Writing Center is busy this month as children make their own valentines. Many children can now read and write "I love you" inside their cards all by themselves. If they cannot, it is on the February word board to copy. Some children can add quite a bit more to their message as they stretch out/sound out the words they want to write. The materials for valentines dominate the Writing Center the first two weeks of February. After Valentine's Day, the children will settle back into copying words for their February Pictionary from the chart or bulletin board in the Writing Center. Words for the pictionary this month can include: love, valentines, hearts, Lincoln, Washington, Martin Luther King, and any other special words the students will be discussing this month. Put a picture above each word so that the children who cannot read the words can still use the pictures and their letter sound knowledge to help them read and write the new February words.

Post Office (Center)

Susan Neuman and Kathleen Roskos ("Literacy Knowledge in Practice: Contexts of Participation for Young Writers and Readers," *Reading Research Quarterly*, Vol. 32, No. 1, 1997, pp. 10-32) write about using authentic play settings for your students to learn about reading and writing. The "centers" they suggest help children use reading and writing for real reasons.

One suggestion, which would fit nicely into your February activities, is a post office that has paper, stationery, envelopes, pencils, markers, rubber stamps, stamp pad, signs, play money, etc. (Use heart stickers for stamps.) Children could make and mail valentines to their parents or guardians this month. Provide each student with an index card on which you have written his or her mailing address. The student can then copy the address down on the front of an envelope.

Michelle

Mr. & Mrs. Hall
3060 Their Street
Winston-Salem, NC 27106

ASSESSING PROGRESS

Continue to help your students who did not master all the tasks on the January assessment. Call upon the children who did not know the days of the week and weather words during the opening, giving them lots of repetition so they can learn these words. Ask the children who could not read their classmates' names to help pass back student papers so that they get practice with the names. Continue to read rhyming books and assist the children who need extra help with the concept of rhyme. When it is time to talk about familiar words in a new big book, have the whole class listen for how many beats are in the words and then clap those beats. You may want to call on students to clap the beats individually, focusing on the children who needed help with this particular skill.

Use the "Concepts of Print Checklist" when children are reading big books or predictable charts. Ask the children to point to the words as they read. Then, ask the children if they can show just one word, and then ask them to point to the first and last letters of that word. If the children are successful in this task, make a note on their assessment sheet.

Some children may need individual attention for the remainder of the year. Knowing who these children are and the tasks they need to practice will allow you to give them little snatches of instruction as they engage in classroom and center activities along with everyone else. Remember, good teachers never give up on their students!

Will March come in like a lion or a lamb? Will it be windy and cold or will it be warm and spring-like? March is a wonderful month to see a wide variety of weather in most parts of the country. Many children now look forward to warmer days, playing outside, and watching the landscape turn green. Predicting the weather is almost impossible, but watching and charting the weather can be fun!

THE OPENING

As you talk about the days of the week, the month, and the date, it is time to call on those "late bloomers" in kindergarten who now know all the answers. Listen to their answers when you ask these questions: "What do you notice?" and "How do you know?" You will see how much they have learned since entering your kindergarten class. It is also time to reflect upon what your students have learned and what else you may need to do to prepare your students to be successful in first grade.

- Can most of the class count to 100?

- Can most of your students look at words and crosscheck them by their beginning sounds?

- Do they know what comes before and after each day of the week and each month of the year?

- Can they find the correct weather word?

- Can they place the tally mark beside the right word on the weather chart?

- Can they think of words that begin like the tongue twister on the board?

- Do they choose to read and write in centers and also when they have free time at home and at school?

- When you write the morning message, do the children want to help you and are their spelling attempts becoming more correct?

- Can they stretch out words, listen for the sounds, and notice more sound patterns and familiar spelling patterns?

- Does the opening go quickly and smoothly, even though you have added more to it since the beginning of the year?

When you answer each of these questions, you will see how far the majority of your students have come. **The important question is: "Have all children made progress on the journey toward literacy?" It is not important that all children be at the same place in this journey.**

When children come to you with all different levels of literacy, you are doing a good job if you accept them where they are and help them move forward in their learning.

READING ALOUD TO CHILDREN

A favorite book to read to young children is *We're Going on a Bear Hunt* by Michael Rosen (Harper Collins,1993). For children who have been stuck inside for the long winter, going on a bear hunt sounds like fun! As the students listen to this repetitive story, ask them to imagine going through splashy, sploshy water and squelch, squerch mud with their family, and then being fortunate enough to find a BEAR! The students have fun pretending to race home and trying to remember which way to run.

Each member of your class still may be working on their own alphabet book from February. Another alphabet book to read and enjoy this month is *Potluck* by Anne Shelby (Scott Foresman, 1993). In the story, everybody is coming for a potluck dinner. "Edmund enters with enchiladas, followed by Fran who furnishes fruit." Guess what Lonnie brings? Lasagna! The alliterative text and the illustrations make this book a favorite among children as they try to predict who is coming next with what. They have a hint—because it is an alphabet book.

A good multicultural book that you can read to your class is *Grandma's Helper* by Lois Meyer (Scott Foresman, 1993). A little girl helps her grandma shop by translating her grandma's Spanish into English. Together they buy bread, milk, stamps, and oranges. This is another book with repetitive patterns, good illustrations, and a bonus—a focus on Spanish.

READING WITH CHILDREN— Shared Reading with Predictable Big Books

Since March is a good month to watch and chart the weather, it is also a good month to read a book about the weather. One such book is *What Will the Weather Be Like Today?* by Paul Rogers (Scholastic, 1989). This informational book is all about the weather and animals in many different places asking the same question, "What will the weather be like today?" The animals wonder, "Will it be windy? Will it be warm?" just as the children in your class do each day. The book ends with the familiar question, "How is the weather where you are today?"

Read and Talk About the Book

For the first and second readings of this book, you should focus on the information in the book and discuss it. The book is full of information and each page is a story in itself. The book has wonderful illustrations that will help children talk about the different places, the different kinds of weather, and where this weather would be found. Does your area have all these types of weather? Why or why not? This book has information for children who have not experienced a wide variety of weather.

Encourage the Children to Join in the Reading

The pictures make the book predictable in places and the rhyming words help in other parts. Once children have had the book read to them several times, they will begin to use the pictures and print and chime in to "share" the reading. When they see the pictures of kites, sailboats, and hair blowing they know to say, "Will it be windy?" The next picture is a summer day so they will ask, "Will it be warm?" and so forth.

Act It Out

This book does not lend itself to acting out, but it does lend itself to lots of discussion. You could play charades, a game in which the weather word to be guessed is pantomimed by the children. Children could show how one acts on a cold day, windy day, or rainy day. This is fun and a learning experience!

Make the Book Available

Remember that children want their favorite books read over and over, then they pretend they can read them, and eventually, they will be able to read them! Be sure to put this big book and/or the little book version in the Reading Center for children to enjoy as they are learning more about the weather.

WRITING WITH CHILDREN— Predictable Charts

March is known as the windy month, and a weather unit on the wind, reading a book about the wind, or talking about the wind can lead to a predictable chart about all the things the wind can blow.

The Wind Blew

The wind blew a balloon. (Adam)

The wind blew a kite. (Paul)

The wind blew an umbrella. (Michelle)

The wind blew the leaves. (Emily)

The wind blew my hair. (Suzanne)

The wind blew ...

Another predictable chart to write in March is about kites. Kites are fun to fly on a windy day in the school yard or in a nearby field or park. Sometimes parents will help you with this project. Young children like to see the wind lift the kite up, up, up in the air. After watching a kite fly and talking about the wind and kites, ask your students, "Where would you go if you were a kite? Where would you fly to?" Their answers will tell you about the places they would like to visit.

A Kite Story

I would fly to Paris. (Erica)

I would fly to the beach. (Michelle)

I would fly to a hospital. (Adam)

I would fly to Florida. (Ryan)

I would fly to Disneyworld. (Suzanne)

I would fly to Washington, D. C. (William)

I would fly to space. (Refugio)

I would fly to New York. (Jasmine)

I would fly to the beach. (Olivia)

I would fly to India. (Nikki)

I would fly to Hawaii. (Mike)

I would fly to my Grandma's. (Paul)

I would fly to my friends. (Mitchell)

- Ask each child to come to the front of the classroom and point to each word (track print) in the sentence as he or she reads it.

- Give the children their sentences to cut apart. (Do not do this any longer for the students unless one or two of them still need this kind of support.)

- After they cut the sentences into words, have the students place the words on their papers.

- Check to make sure the word order is correct.

- Then, have the children paste the words down on their papers.

- Let the children illustrate their sentences.

Most students can now draw quite well, especially kites, and when the book is put together, it is both lovely and fun to read.

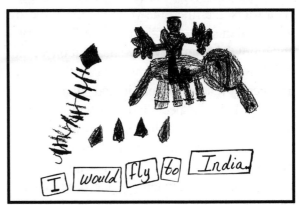

DEVELOPING PHONEMIC AWARENESS— Rhyming Books

Mem Fox is an author known for creating picture books with a strong sense of repetition, like *Hattie and the Fox* (Simon & Schuster, 1988), or rhythm and rhyme, like *Koala Lou* (Harcourt Brace, 1994). She has another rhyming book titled *Zoo-looking* (Mondo, 1995) that kindergarten children love. This book comes in both little and big book sizes. It is a story about a little girl named Flora. Flora and her father go to the zoo one day. Flora not only looks at the animals, but the animals look back! One animal has a snack, another gets a whack, and so on. Before you go very far into this book, the students will be listening for the rhymes.

Read and Talk About the Book

This book is written in rhyme so that children can listen to it, join in, and share the reading. As always, the first time you read the book to your students, let them just listen to the story and enjoy it. After they have heard it once, the students will want to chant along with you on the second reading or join in and share the reading. This is especially true if you have the big book version and the children can see the pictures and print easily. Talk about the animals at the zoo—which ones are familiar to your kindergarten students (tiger, bear, snake, monkey) and which ones are not familiar

(penguin, ostrich, koala). How many penguins or koalas are in the city streets, on a rural farm, or in their neighborhoods? Reading is a way of introducing young children to things they have not seen before.

Act It Out

Kindergarten students prove they are natural actors and have a good time acting out this story. After choosing two students to be Flora (a girl) and her father (a boy), the remainder of the characters are the zoo animals in the story. There are several animals at the zoo, so each child can have a turn if you act out the story two or three times. Each zoo animal can be drawn or copied on a piece of white construction paper. Once again, laminate the drawings, punch two holes at the top, tie lengths of yarn through the holes, and have the children wear these cards around their necks so that everyone will know which characters they are.

Reread the story and let the children look at each other just as Flora and the zoo animals did during this day at the zoo. How does a snake slither through a crack? How does a bear gobble up a snack? Flora and her father can smile at each other, but her father does not have to pick her up —as he does in the picture in the story. When children act out stories, they have fun, but it also helps students understand the story (comprehension). Having Flora look at each animal at the zoo, one by one, also helps the children understand the "sequence" of the story (what happened first, next, last, etc.).

Once the book has been read, enjoyed, reread, and acted out, most children can read or pretend read the book. Make the big book or little book version that you read to the class available in the Reading Center so that the students can enjoy this book again and again.

Rounding Up the Rhymes

Read the story again another day. Children do not get tired of listening to Mem Fox's story because of its rhythm and rhyme. Ask the students to listen for the rhyming words in the story. If you have been reading rhymes and talking about rhyming words, this should be an easy task for them!

• Read the story again and ask the students to help you "round up the rhymes" (the words that rhyme with *back*). The children easily find *black, crack, smack, whack, snack, yak,* and lots of *backs*.

• Write the rhyming words on the chalkboard or on a piece of chart paper, one by one, as you and the children find them in the story.

• Then, ask, "What do you notice?" See if the children notice the same spelling pattern in all the words except *yak*.

Most of the time, but not always, words that rhyme with *back* are spelled with the same spelling pattern *a-c-k*.

Making Words

Work on phonemic awareness with your students by doing the "making words" activity. Using the laminated cards you made earlier or the bright yellow vinyl letter vests you purchased (see February), the children can "become" letters. Choose three students, one for the *a* card/vest, one for the *c* card/vest, and one for the *k* card/vest to become the *ack* rhyme or spelling pattern. Choose other children to be the letters *b, p, J, r, s, Z, m, n,* and *c*. Let the children whose cards spell *b, a, c,* and *k* stand in front of the class. Say the letters *b-a-c-k* aloud and the word "back." Take away the *b* by having that student sit down and say aloud what is left—"ack." Have the other letters come up and stand with *a-c-k*. Let the students notice that it is important that they stand in front of *a-c-k*. See which of the other students can read the new words as the children who are holding letter cards or wearing letter vests come to the front of the classroom and join *a-c-k* to become a new word, such as *Jack, pack, rack, sack, tack, crack, smack,* or *snack.*

This manipulation of letters and sounds to make new words is an important part of learning to read. Making words is a wonderful way to introduce your class to the concept known as "onset and rime." Young children understand things they can "see," and being the letters and making words is an excellent way for children to "see" how beginning sounds and spelling patterns come together to make many different words. It also helps the students to see how changing a letter can change the word!

WRITING BY CHILDREN

Writing continues to be an area where children constantly improve. As they learn more about letters, sounds, and words, the students' writing and spelling skills show growth. Since they are discussing kites and the wind, many of the students choose to write stories about kites during writing activities and their time at the Writing Center. Continue to model a story for your students and think aloud as you write. Model how to use the color words that are up in the room to help you as you write the story. Stretch out the long words and listen for all the sounds you can hear. Talk as you write.

"If I were a kite, I would be purple and yellow so everyone could see me. I would fly in the sky. I would fly to my mother's house and see all my friends."

The children follow your lead, and they choose their favorite colors ("I am red"). They fly to their favorite places ("I would fly to school"). They tell about the things they see ("I saw a plan"). You may notice in some of the students' responses that they do not know about silent e's yet! **The children stretch out their words and write the sounds they hear ("pe..pl"). You can read the child's writing and so can the child that wrote it! As the children write, continue to praise their attempts and coach them so that they may become even better writers.**

Modeling how to write and thinking aloud as you write, along with coaching the children with their first stories, really pays off. It is almost impossible to believe that these are the same students that were drawing pictures and copying words when you first asked them to write at the beginning of the school year!

Ashley

I would fly to New York City.

I saw the world.

I am red and gray.

I saw people.

Nathan

I would fly to Washington, D.C.

My kite is red and blue.

I saw a plane.

CENTERS

Reading Center

The Reading Center is filled with many ABC books, including the books that the class made. Children are now spending time reading their favorite books—usually ones they can actually read. Pretend reading still happens but children know when they pick a book whether they will be able to really read it or if they are just going to enjoy the pictures and pretend to read it. It is somewhat amazing that kindergarten students can accurately assess their reading ability with each book they pick up.

Read several new books and then add them to your Reading Center. Add weather books and books about the wind, along with any leprechaun stories you have collected. Children love to hear leprechaun stories around St. Patrick's Day. Sometimes, you may have to focus on the Easter and/or Passover holidays during March as well. That would mean more "bunny" and "egg" books to read, and even more books to share with the students and place in the Reading Center.

Writing Center

As kindergarten students learn more about writing and get better at doing it, the Writing Center becomes more popular than ever. The computer is a favorite piece of equipment. Students have discovered that it makes writing their stories much easier, and handwriting is no longer a problem. Along with copying the March Pictionary chart or bulletin board, the students can write letters to people they know and notes to their friends. If you have a commercial pictionary, put it in the Writing

Center. Some students may want to check the spelling of words they write in their notes that just do not look right to them.

Travel Agency or Doctor's Office (Center)

In February, we added a post office to our centers. March is a good month to have a travel agency for all those places the students want their kites to go. What would you put in a travel agency (posters, calendar, computer, paper, pencils, markers, travel brochures, etc.)?

Another possibility is a doctor's office or health clinic. This center could have an appointment book, pencil, markers, calendar, note pad, play money, insurance forms, file folders, clipboard, eye chart, doctor's bag, stethoscope, etc. Children could pretend to be a patient, a doctor, a nurse, or a secretary. What fun the students could have reading (or pretend reading) and writing (or pretend writing) for real reasons!

ASSESSING PROGRESS

March marks the end of the third quarter in many schools. It is time once again to look at the progress these students have made in kindergarten. **Assessment is not something that you do only every quarter, but something that you do daily as you kidwatch and take note of each child's progress.** Assessing this progress involves looking at the names and words children know and looking at their phonemic awareness and how it is developing. As we discussed under the section on rhyming, phonemic awareness is the ability to manipulate words. It includes knowing that the sentence

I had a bad day at school today.

has a lot more words than the sentence

I got mad.

Phonemic awareness also includes being able to clap syllables in words and knowing that the word *automobile* takes more claps than the word *car*. Perhaps the most critical phonemic awareness ability to assess towards the end of kindergarten is the ability to come up with a word that rhymes with another word. Children who have phonemic awareness can tell you that *bike* rhymes with *Mike* and that *book* does not rhyme with *Mike*. Assess this phonemic awareness by observing the student's ability to do rhyming word tasks as you are doing activities with the whole class. As you go into April, most children will have the desired level of phonemic awareness, and you will need to know which students need continued nudges toward developing this.

Our "new" assessment this quarter will focus on letter/sound knowledge. Many children have learned some letter names and sounds. Some children can recognize all 26 letters of the alphabet and know the sounds these letters make in words. Other children usually recognize all 26 letters in both upper and lower case and have learned the names and sounds for the most common letters. Usually, the letter names and sounds children know are based on those words which they can read and write. Students typically know the letters in their name and the names of their friends.

Assessment of Letter Sounds

To assess students' letter/sound knowledge, say the words listed below and let the students write the letters they hear at the beginning and ending of each word on the space provided. Notice that the vowel is written so that the child does not have to worry about this part of the word—our focus is on beginning and ending consonants only.

Call 3-5 children to a table at the side or back of your classroom or in the Writing Center, so they can do this task at the same time. Give each child a piece of paper like the one shown at right (or duplicate page 87) and say:

> "I will say a word. Then, I want you to say the word with me. Write down the sounds you hear at the beginning and the end of the word on the lines."

    1. ham

    2. rat

    3. fan

    4. pad

    5. bag

Be sure the children are saying each word as they try to write the letters that make the sounds.

Name _____

Date _____

b   d   f   g   h   m   n   p   r   t

1. _____ a _____

2. _____ a _____

3. _____ a _____

4. _____ a _____

5. _____ a _____

Name_____

Date_____

b   d   f   g   h   m   n   p   r   t

1. _____ a _____

2. _____ a _____

3. _____ a _____

4. _____ a _____

5. _____ a _____

(See page 86 for directions.)

Spring is finally here! The warmer days are pleasant signs of what is coming. Many students have a spring holiday and a spring break to anticipate. There is a lot to learn at school and within the community. You can see flowers and trees blooming and trees and grass turning green. Planting season begins in many areas. Baby animals are being born and signs of new life are everywhere. It is your job as a kindergarten teacher to help your students see the changes and understand what is happening in their world and why.

THE OPENING

Who is at school today? Is anyone absent? What day of the week is it? What is the month? date? year? How many days have you been in school? Can anyone count them? Let's make a mark (or tally mark) for each day. A straw is added to the jar. The straws have been grouped into bundles of ten and then a hundreds bundle, and the children count along with the teacher. Count the "hundreds" first, the "tens" next, and then the "ones" to find out for sure how many days the students have been in school. The calendar for April is on the bulletin board where the students can see it as you talk about the now-familiar days of the week, the date, and then chart the weather each day of the month.

Once again you can draw the children's attention to the beginning of words on the calendar and the bulletin board by asking familiar questions like:

"Can you find the word *Tuesday* on the calendar?"

"How do you know this says *Tuesday*?"

"What do you notice about the word *Tuesday*?"

"How do you know it is not *Thursday*?"

"*Thursday* begins with a *T* also."

Your students will probably tell you that *Thursday* has a *Th* at the beginning. Students who have learned letter names and the sounds they represent at the beginning of words are now ready to listen for more than one sound at the beginning of words.

More Tongue Twisters

Kindergarten teachers often add a few tongue twisters at the end of kindergarten for which some children (but not all) are ready. One Thursday, write the following sentence on the board: Thirsty Thelma is thankful for her thermos. Ask the students what they notice about this tongue twister.

A student answers that many of the words begin with *th*, two letters that make one sound! Ask the children to say the *th* words with you and listen for the *th* sound at the beginning of the words. Are the beginning sounds the same for those words with *th* at the beginning? YES!

This month, you may want to add two letter tongue twisters to your list, such as:

Charlie Chipmunk chooses to chomp cherry cheesecake.

Shawn showed Shirley his shiny new shoes.

Whitney the white whale whistles and whirls.

Thirsty Thelma thinks that's great.

Morning Message

When you write the morning message, you may be aware that it is the children who want to do the thinking and spelling. Many children have things they want to say each morning. When asked to spell the high frequency words, they can! Practice and repetition have made these familiar words for some kindergartners.

When the children are doing most of the work, you know there is a lot of learning going on! Let the children do the spelling of the longer, harder words as you stretch them out. Write exactly what they tell you to write. You will notice that some of the children can spell many words correctly by this time. Even when their spelling is close, do not change it. You want to show your students what people (writers) do when they do not know how to spell a word. They do not change "enormous" to "big" because they cannot spell "enormous" but can spell "big." Instead, the writer writes "enormous" and spells it as best as he or she can. **Coaching your students to invent the spelling of words they do not know pays off. Invented spelling helps these five-year-olds think about how words sound and how they are spelled. Some words will still trick these young students, but there are some words which still trick adults!**

Once the holidays of Passover and Easter have come and gone, spring is the big topic during the month of April. Some children will share their travel plans for spring break. Other children will stay home and enjoy the warm weather and use the break from school to rest up before the fourth and final school quarter. When children talk about their experiences for the morning message, they use their big voices and speak in complete sentences as they have been told to do all year. For some children, the few small words they uttered at the beginning of the kindergarten year have now become long complete sentences that give the other students new information. **Language for many students has improved in kindergarten by talking and listening during the opening each morning.**

READING ALOUD TO CHILDREN

There are many books about spring and the spring holidays of Passover and Easter to read to students. What you read often depends upon the customs in your community. Books about planting a garden and baby animals are also popular with both kindergarten teachers and students. The books you read also depend upon the theme(s) you plan to teach this month.

Popular books for April include:

All about Seeds by Susan Kuchalla (Troll Assoc., 1982)

Carrot Seed, The by Ruth Krauss (HarperCollins, 1945).

Hungry Caterpillar, The by Eric Carle (Scholastic, Inc., 1969, 1987).

I Like Rain by Claude Belanger (Shortland Publication, 1988).

It Looked Like Spilt Milk by Charles G. Shaw (Harper Trophy, 1988).

It's Spring! by Else H. Minarik (Greenwillow Books, 1989).

Over in the Meadow by Sharon O'Neil (Harcourt, Brace, Jovanovich, 1989).

Vegetable Garden by Douglas Floring (Harcourt Brace, 1991).

CHILDREN READING BY THEMSELVES— Self-Selected Reading

After your daily read aloud time, let the entire class read for a few minutes. A good way to get ready for this activity is to prepare four or five "book buckets." These are usually dish pans filled with books—familiar books that have been read to the class, easy, predictable "beginning readers," old favorites like Dr. Seuss, and books on your current theme. **It is called "self-selected" reading because children can choose the books they want to read at this time and there is no follow-up activity.**

• Let the children sit at their seats or find a comfortable place in the room to read.

• The time period for your students to read depends upon how long they will read independently. Most kindergarten teachers begin with five minutes and then later lengthen the time period. A kitchen timer can help make this activity easier for you. Tell the children how many minutes they can spend reading today, then set your timer.

• Invite the students to read silently until they hear the timer go off. Most children need a quiet place to read, so it is important to start with a small amount of time and encourage the children to be as quiet as possible.

- Circulate around the room visiting several students and listening to them as they read a few lines to you.

- Talk about the books they are reading. What is happening in the story? What do they think will happen next? Why?

- When the timer goes off, ask the children to put their books back into the "book buckets." Along with the books in the "book buckets," you can also let the students read the class-made big books, children's magazines, and magazines brought from home.

> **The purpose of self-selected reading is to let all children have time to read each day so that reading becomes a lifelong habit. This is the time children put into practice those strategies you have taught.**

READING WITH CHILDREN— Shared Reading With Predictable Big Books

April is known as the rainy month. *I Like Rain* by Claude Belanger (Shortland, 1988) is a read-together, sing-together book about the weather. *Rain* by Robert Kalan (Houghton Mifflin, 1996) is a book all about rain and is now available as a big book. In the big book format, it is wonderful for shared reading, with predictable pictures and text. You can also review the color words your children learned at the beginning of the year while reading this book.

Read and Talk About the Book

The first and second readings should focus on the meaning and enjoyment of the book. Read the book to your class; pause occasionally to talk about the pictures and the print (blue sky, yellow sun, white clouds, gray clouds, gray sky). Reread the story and help your students notice the repeating pattern: Rain on (color word) (object). Do they notice that the "rain" in the picture is really the word "rain?" How does this story end? Have they ever seen a rainbow after it rains? Many kindergarten children have never seen a rainbow, but are fascinated by them. After reading this story, young children will begin to look up in the sky after it rains to see if they can find a rainbow!

Encourage the Children to Join in the Reading

After you have read the book to the children, let them "echo-read" the pages by repeating the words after you. Another way to reread the book is to have your students join in the reading. Assign a color for each child (blue, yellow, white, gray, red, orange, brown, purple, white, green) and let the child read the page(s) with his or her color words on it. All children love to join in and share the reading once the rain begins ("Rain on the green grass" and "Rain on the black road"). Whichever way you choose, either letting one child read the page or the entire class, the children love to see and say "RAINBOW" at the end.

Act It Out

The children can act out the story if they are given cards with the different colors to hold in front of them or to wear around their necks with yarn ties of the same color.

Blue says, "Blue sky."

Yellow says, "Yellow sun."

White says, "White clouds."

Gray says, "Gray clouds."

Then, when the rain comes, the children who are the other colors say their parts:

Green says, "Rain on the green grass."

Black says, "Rain on the black roads."

At the end, all the children can stand and say, "RAINBOW!"

Make the Book Available

When children hear and enjoy a book which you have read to the whole class, they like to pick it up by themselves later on and enjoy it again. Because of the pictures and color words, *Rain* is an easy story for some students to read by themselves. The pictures make pretend reading easier for those who are still at that stage. Sometimes you may see several children sit down together with a book and help each other read it. Listen to their prompts to each other—you will hear yourself! Young children learn to do what they see. If the students see you circulating and helping children reread books, they will want to do the same.

SHARED WRITING— Predictable Charts

Predictable charts lead to more class books, and both spring and rain are good topics for another predictable chart. After reading the book *Where Does the Butterfly Go When It Rains?* by May Gorelick (Mondo, 1997), the children will be ready to tell you where they think the butterfly will go. Take a piece of chart paper and write the title of the book at the top of the page. Write the children's responses to the question.

Where Does the Butterfly Go When it
Rains?

. . . in a tree. (Ryan)

. . . in a hole. (Adam)

. . . in a bush. (William)

. . . under a branch. (Olivia)

. . . flies to his home. (Michelle)

. . . in the grass. (Mitchell)

. . . under a basket. (Suzanne)

. . . in a tree. (Refugio)

. . . under a box. (Paul)

. . . in a flower. (Jasmine)

. . . under a chair. (Emily)

. . . someplace sunny. (Richard)

. . . under a porch. (Rayshaun)

. . . in a cocoon. (Nikki)

. . . in a window. (Julie)

. . . to live with other bugs. (Jimmy)

. . . under someplace. (Tiara)

. . . in a house. (Erica)

. . . under a leaf. (Mike)

. . . in a tent. (Jacob)

Sentence Builders

Ask the children to come to the chart one at a time and "touch read" their sentences. The following day, have several of the sentences from this chart written on sentence strips and then cut the sentences into words. Take the words of one sentence and give them to the students. Let the children "find their place" as they build each sentence. Ask the first and last student, "Why are you standing at the beginning (or end) of the sentence?" See if the first student can tell you that the capital letter at the beginning of his or her word helped determine where he or she would stand. Likewise, see if the last student can tell you that the period at the end of his or her word showed him or her where to stand. After each sentence is "built" by the children standing in the right order with their words in front of them, read the words aloud so the rest of the class can check to see if the sentence is correct.

Making a Class Book

After several sentences have been built, it is time for each child to cut apart the words in his or her own sentence and then put the words back in the right order. Check to see that each word is in the correct place in each child's sentence before you allow the children to paste the words onto sheets of drawing paper. Some students may still need help with this, but others will find it a simple task. Finally, ask the students to illustrate their sentences. The children should draw a big butterfly and the place they think the butterfly will go if it rains. The children can also draw rain in the picture. After the children have finished illustrating their sentences, help them to put the class book "in order" by lining up with their pages, using the predictable chart as a guide. Add front and back covers to the pages using colored construction paper. Write the title of the class book on the front cover in thick black magic marker. Draw a nice big butterfly on the front, or cut one out of a magazine and paste it on the front cover. Now you have another book that most of the children can read to add to your collection.

Another book that lends itself to making a predictable chart is *What's In My Pocket?* by Rozanne Lanczak Williams (Creative Teaching Press, 1995). After reading and enjoying the book, you can make a predictable chart with the children as they answer the question "What's In My Pocket?" All of their responses should begin with "In my pocket is...."

ENVIRONMENTAL PRINT—Cereals

If children are to improve their reading and writing skills and word knowledge, they must have practice. Some children see the people who live in their homes reading books and magazines and writing on a daily basis. Other children do not have books and magazines at home. We want children to "practice" at home some of the things we do in school.

One way to do this is to use environmental print. Most children know their favorite cereal, drink, and fast-food restaurant. Many children (and adults) who cannot actually read can still recognize the logo of the products they see and use on a daily basis. So, if you want children to practice letter names, teach them by using the cereal boxes that are found in their homes. Bring in several boxes from different types of popular cereal (or have the students bring in empty boxes). Talk about cereal and see how many students eat it for breakfast each day. Graph the class's favorite cereals and see which brands/types are the most popular.

Start with the class's favorite brand of cereal. Hold up the box and have the children look at it. Talk about the colors and the pictures on the box. Have the children count the letters in the cereal name with you (For example, if the class favorite was Cheerios™, you would count "1-2-3-4-5-6-7-8. There are 8 letters in *Cheerios*."). Then, have the children say the letter names with you ("C-h-e-e-r-i-o-s").

Next, pass out laminated letter cards. The letters should be identical to the letters on the box. Ask, "Who has the C? h? e? e? r? i? o? s?" Have the children come to the front of the class and stand in the right order. Point to each child holding a laminated letter card individually and have him or her say the letter name on the card. Then, collect the letters and have the children return to their seats.

Cheerios™ is being used by permission of General Mills, Inc.

Holding the box up again, ask, "What do you notice about the box?" You may hear responses like

> "*Cheerios* begins with a capital *C*."
>
> "The box is yellow."
>
> " *Cheerios* begins like *Charles*."
>
> " There is an *o* in *Cheerios*."
>
> "*Cheerios* ends with an *s*."

After discussing the box, the brand name, and the letters, place the laminated letters in the pocket chart to form the word *Cheerios*. Let the students write the word *Cheerios* on pieces of drawing paper with black crayons or black markers, and then have them draw a picture of the box.

Once you have done several types of cereals, you know that children will have a place to practice letter names each morning at the breakfast table. Young children enjoy showing off what they have learned in school and cereal boxes are found in most homes.

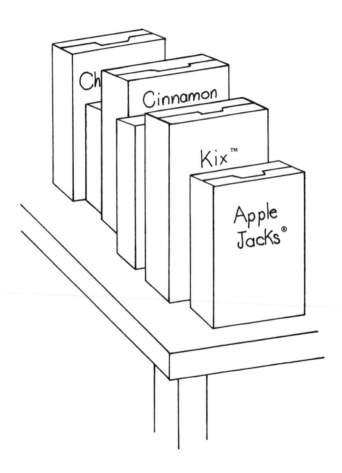

WRITING BY CHILDREN

Writing continues to be an area where children constantly improve as they learn more about letters and sounds. The words that the students are writing and spelling show this growth. Since April is the time to discuss spring and rain, the children often choose to write stories about those subjects during their writing time or when they are in the Writing Center. Continue to model stories and "think aloud" as you write on a piece of chart paper or on the chalkboard. Stretch out the long words and have the students listen for all the sounds they can hear. Talk as you write:

"It is Spring. (*Spring* is on the bulletin board, and I can copy it from there.)

The weather is warm and sunny. (*Warm* and *sunny* are words we use many mornings. I can find weather words listed near where we do the opening each morning.)

The grass is green. (*Green* is a color word, and I see it written over there.)

The trees are green. (I can find *green* in the sentence above.)

We can play outside and have fun!"

The children will follow your lead. When it rains, many children will write about the rain. The children tell about the things they see; they stretch out their words and write the sounds they hear in words. As the children write, continue to coach them and praise their attempts.

In kindergarten, celebrate what each child can do, especially what they can do when they write. Do not ask five- and six-year-olds to spell correctly—they cannot! If you ask them to use only words they know how to spell correctly, you will not see the same growth in their writing and spelling skills. It is a good idea to share each child's growth with the child's parents by showing them writing samples collected from their child throughout the year. Most kindergarten parents are amazed at their child's writing—they never wrote in kindergarten! Some parents may need to be reassured that the children will learn to edit stories and begin to work on the correct spelling of high frequency words in the first grade.

Jaleel

My mom lived in Africa.
Africa is a fun place.
What kinds of masks are there?
There are lions in Africa.
There are monkeys in Africa.
Egypt is in Africa.
Did you know that there are sights in Africa?
I wish I could go to Africa.

Africa

My mom livd in Afroco.
Afroco is a fon plas.
Wot kins of masks r thair?
Thair is liens in Afroco.
Thair or mnnecis in Afroco.
Ejip is in Afroco.
Did you no that thair r sites in Afroco?
I wish I cod go to Afroco.

Jaleel

Sam

I have a pet.
It is a dog.
I like her a lot.
I lay with my dog.
I play with my dog.
I lay with my dog at night.
I read her dog books.
I take her to the vet.
I love my dog.

My Pet

I have a pet.
It is a dog.
I like hr a lot.
I lay waf my dog.
I play waf my dog.
I lay waf my dog at nit.
I red hr dog books.
I tac hr to the vat.
I love my dog.

Sam

If you are lucky enough to have a computer lab at your school with time available for kindergarten classes to go there, take advantage of it! Some kindergarten classes go into the computer lab each day for their writing time. Let children write either at the computers or at the desks or tables. Everyone writes, and at the end of this writing time, several children get to share what they wrote in an "Author's Chair" format. **Sharing stories gives these young authors new writing ideas as they hear topics that are familiar to them. It also gives the children another audience for their work besides you.**

CENTERS

Reading Center

The centers are tied more closely to the themes you are studying at this time of year. Since the children are studying about spring and plants this month, books and stories about plants and growing vegetables are found in the Reading Center. You can also begin placing signs in each center telling the children what to do. When some children can read the signs, they will help the other children who cannot.

Writing Center

You might want to put materials in the Writing Center so that children can make signs for their gardens at home. The April Pictionary chart or bulletin board has words for the parts of a plant. Children enjoy using a computer in the Writing Center because they can write so much more when they use it. Make sure that all children get a turn at writing on the computer in the Writing Center—some students may try to monopolize the computer.

Grocery Store (Center)

In April, you can add a grocery store center and expand your study of environmental print. Use cereal boxes and other familiar grocery items to help students learn about letters. Place empty cans and boxes of food in the center. (Make sure there are no sharp edges on the cans or boxes!) You may also include a cash register, play money, a basket or small push cart, pads for grocery lists, and bags. Students can pretend to be the cashier, the bagger, or the customer who can buy whatever he or she needs or wants!

ASSESSING PROGRESS

As we go into the last months of kindergarten, most children will have the desired level of phonemic awareness. You have been working on letter names and letter sounds in the way that most children learn these concepts—by talking about words and letters and sounds. You know which children need extra help to continue to develop this skill.

Assessing Letter Sounds

Our assessment last month focused on letter/sound knowledge. To assess this knowledge once more, we will do a similar task. Call 3-5 children to a table at the side or the back of your classroom, or into a center, so that they can do this task at the same time. Give each child a piece of paper like the example shown at right (or duplicate one or more of the following pages). Notice that the vowel is written so that each child need only to focus on the beginning and ending consonants.

Name_____

Date_____

b d f g h m n p r t w

1. ____i____

2. ____i____

3. ____i____

4. ____i____

5. ____i____

Say to the students: "I will say a word. Then, I want you to say the word with me. Write down the sounds you hear at the beginning and the end of the word on the lines."

1. pin	1. mud
2. rib	2. rut
3. big	3. bun
4. hid	4. cup
5. fin	5. tub

Name_____

Date_____

b d f g h m n p r t w

1. ____i____

2. ____i____

3. ____i____

4. ____i____

5. ____i____

(See page 99 for directions.)

Name_____

Date_____

b d f g h m n p r t w

1. _____u_____

2. _____u_____

3. _____u_____

4. _____u_____

5. _____u_____

(See page 99 for directions.)

The end of the year is in sight! Many teachers wonder if they will get it all done—if they will finish all the things they wanted to accomplish this year. For most the answer is "yes," but they still worry. Why? **Teachers never see the job of teaching and learning as fully accomplished! You see a portion of the task completed each year, but no child has accomplished all of which he or she is capable. There is so much to learn that it takes a lifetime, not one year in kindergarten.**

Some students are sad that the school year is coming to an end—they will miss the teacher whom they have come to respect and love. Other children will miss their new friends that do not live close by and who they will not see again until the next school year. Some kindergarten children also worry about going to first grade and who their first grade teacher will be!

If you have been doing multilevel activities as described, then you know that most of your students are ready for first grade and those about whom you were most worried have come the farthest. As a kindergarten teacher, you cannot make up five years of literacy learning in one year, but you can narrow the gap and get your students on the road to learning by providing them with the same experiences that children who come from literate homes have had. That is what the activities in the previous chapters were meant to do.

If you have been doing multilevel activities and accepting all the approximations that different students make, all of your students should have moved forward. If not, you must look carefully at their attempts and your attitude. Are you providing the support each student needs in his/her literacy learning? Are your expectations within their limits? Are you celebrating their successes? **KINDERGARTEN TEACHERS WHO BELIEVE THAT ALL CHILDREN CAN LEARN USUALLY HAVE CLASSES WHERE ALL CHILDREN DO LEARN!**

THE OPENING

The opening continues to the very last day of school. This is a time to celebrate how well your students can do with the opening tasks. The familiar questions were not familiar at one time. The children now know the days of the week, the date, and the weather. They can read many of these words. Your students also know with what letter a word begins and several other words that begin with that same letter. They know about rhyming words and how changing a beginning sound can change a word. They have phonemic awareness and are ready for any phonics instruction they may get in first grade. They are also ready for many of the reading and writing tasks they will be asked to do in the coming year. These young children have learned to think about words and how words work, and this will continue in first grade. Tongue twisters, morning messages, and new books are still part of the opening as students continue to listen for and talk about letters and letter sounds.

As the counting gets closer to 180 days (or however many days your school system considers as a school year), kindergarten classes discuss the many events that happen as the year ends—field trips, class picnics, field day, awards day, etc. You should also discuss a few new activities that the class is going to do to prepare for the transition to first grade. These activities are discussed so that children will be aware of why the routine is changing and what will be expected of them as they get ready for first grade. It will also help to make the beginning of the year easier when these same students enter first grade in the fall.

READING ALOUD TO CHILDREN

There are lots of books about flowers, bugs, and summer activities to read to the children. With the year coming to an end, it is also a good time to read classroom favorites. Ask the children about their favorite stories, books, and authors. Graph their favorites and see which books they remember and enjoyed. *Bright Eyes, Brown Skin* by Cheryl Hudson and Bernette G. Ford (Just Us Books, 1990) is a book about four new school friends. The children in the story love to do some of the same things your students have done at school this year—draw, dance, clap, read, dress-up, and play make-believe. Discuss the illustrations in the book and listen for the rhymes.

Popular books for May/June:

Animal Mothers by Atsushi Komori (Putnam & Grossett, 1983).

Berenstain Bears Go To Camp by Stan & Jan Berenstain (Random House, 1982).

City Mouse-Country Mouse (Aesop) pictures by John Wallner (Scholastic, Inc., 1989).

Dibble and Dabble by Dave and Julie Saunders (Scott Foresman, 1996).

Gunnywolf, The retold by Antoinette Delaney (Scott Foresman, 1996).

Have You Seen My Cat? by Eric Carle (Putnam & Grosset, 1988).

Horrible Black Bug, The by Toni Jacquier (Rigby, 1988).

I Know an Old Lady Who Swallowed a Fly illustrated by Slug Signorino (Scott Foresman, 1996).

Living Things by Judith Holloway (Modern Curriculum Press, 1990).

On the Go by Ann Morris (Scott Foresman, 1996).

Very Busy Spider, The by Eric Carle (Putnam & Grosset, 1988).

Wonder of Plants and Flowers, The by Laura Davon (Troll Assoc., 1990).

SELF-SELECTED READING

After your daily read-aloud time, let the entire class read for 10-15 minutes from books you have selected and placed in your "book buckets." **The books the children chose as their favorites are the ones to have available, so the students can "visit" with them one more time before school is out for the summer. Book buckets always contain books that are both fiction (favorite stories) and fact (informational books from which the students can learn).** Young children, just like adults, have a favorite genre (poetry, fairy tales, non-fiction, etc.), so some students will naturally prefer one type of book over a different type. If you have read a variety of books during your daily read-aloud sessions, then you know that the children have been exposed to many kinds of books.

The children should select their book(s) and either sit at their seats or find a comfortable place in the room to read. Continue to remind the children to read quietly to themselves until they hear the timer go off ! Most kindergarten children read with their lips as well as their eyes, but the whisper reading helps them comprehend what they are reading and does not disrupt other children's learning.

As you are circulating around the room, you will notice that most children are reading. Visit with the few students who may need your help to do this task correctly. As you listen to the children read, talk about the book they have chosen.

- What is happening in the story?

- What does the student think will happen next and why?

- Why did he or she choose this particular book?

- What other books has the class read that are like this book?

- What other books has the student read by this author?

- What is his or her favorite part of the book?

- Can the student show you that page?

This "one-on-one" time with each child is important for beginning readers. It is a time to talk about books with your students and to get to know your students better.

READING WITH CHILDREN— Shared Reading With Predictable Big Books

May and June are usually warm and sunny, with days that give a hint of the summer months to come. May has Mother's Day and June has Father's Day—if you go to school that late in June! A good book for shared reading around Mother's Day is *Animal Mothers* by Atsushi Komori (Putnam & Grossett, 1983). *On the Go* by Ann Morris (previously cited) is a story of a trip around the world told in photographs. This nonfiction book has bicycles, horses, buses, trains, boats, cars, planes, and rockets—everything young children know or need to know about the way people go.

Another book that is fun to read and meets all the criteria for shared reading in kindergarten is *Me Too!* by Mercer Mayer (Houghton Mifflin, 1996). It is the story of a brother who tells of the many things he does and his little sister who is always yelling, "Me too!" What does the brother do? He helps his little sister to do the things he is doing.

Read and Talk About the Book With a "Picture Walk"

The first reading of *Me Too!* should focus on the meaning and enjoyment of the book. Talk about the cover, the name of the book, and the author. Can the students read the name of this book? Choose someone to read the name of the book aloud as you point to the words in the title.

The next thing to do is to take a "picture walk" through this book—looking at the pictures and talking about them. Ask the children to predict what happens in this story by looking at what is happening in the pictures. Then, read the book to your class, pausing occasionally to talk about the pictures and the print. Encourage the children to tell what other things the little sister might want to do, just like her brother. Has anyone in your class had this experience with a sister or a brother? Let them tell the class about it.

Encourage the Children to Join in the Reading

Reread the story and encourage your students to join in with the words they know. All the students should join in for the words, "Me Too!" (which are in the word balloons). As you reread the book, pause and allow children to comment on the illustrations and predict what will happen next. Then, turn the page and find out if the children are right. Sometimes, the children will predict correctly; and sometimes, the children are wrong but could have been right. Talk about the predictions and why some are good predictions and why some do not make sense with this story.

Talk about the things that brothers and sisters do together. What time of year is it in each event in the story and how do the students know? Which things can the students do that are in this book? Which things will the students do this summer? Has anyone in the class ever yelled, "Me, too!" to a brother or sister? Has a brother, sister, or friend ever done this to them?

Act It Out

Acting out stories helps children to focus on what is happening in the story. Choose two children to act out each page, or several pairs of children can join in this activity, each pair acting out an event in the book. Another idea is to have two children at a time to pantomime an activity and let the other children find the page the two students are demonstrating.

Make the Book Available

So that your young students can enjoy the book again and again, make the big book available in the Reading Center or put several small books (if you have several copies) in the book buckets. Books that you have read to the class are always favorites for the students to read by themselves during self-selected reading time. Many kindergarten students wonder if they can read these books by themselves—let them have the opportunity to find out! The pictures make pretend reading of this book easier for those children who are still at that stage.

First grade reading usually begins with the shared reading of big books. The big books you have used for shared reading each month and the activities you have provided for your students will prepare them for beginning reading instruction in the first grade.

WRITING WITH CHILDREN— Predictable Charts

After reading the book *Animal Mothers* (previously cited), the children are ready to tell you what they know about mothers and what mothers do besides carrying their babies. On a piece of chart paper, write the title "Happy Mother's Day!" Then, let the children tell you what they think mothers do.

Happy Mother's Day!

Mothers play with you. (Jasmine)

Mothers ride horses with you. (Olivia)

Mothers help you. (Adam)

Mothers cook for you. (Michelle)

Mothers let you have sleepovers. (Emily)

Mothers love you. (Ryan)

Mothers help you clean your room. (William)

Mothers buy you things. (David)

Mothers bake cookies. (Mitchell)

Mothers take you out to eat. (Richard)

Mothers watch TV with you. (Nikki)

Mothers care about you. (Julie)

Mothers read books to you. (Jimmy)

Mothers help you set the table. (Tiara)

Mothers take you to the zoo. (Erica)

Mothers take you to the movies. (Mike)

Mothers take you to baseball practice. (Jacob)

We love our mothers! (Miss Williams)

Another book that lends itself to a predictable chart as kindergarteners are thinking about first grade and being all grown up is *When I Grow Up* by Babs Bell Hajdusiewicz (Dominie Press, 1996). This has rhythm and rhyme. After enjoying the book in the first reading, you can reread it and "Round Up the Rhymes" or write a predictable chart using the sentence "When I Grow Up, I might...."

Sentence Builders

Ask the children to come to the chart, one at a time, and "touch read" their sentences about mothers. The following day, write several of the sentences from this chart on sentence strips and then cut the sentences into words. Take the words of one sentence and let each child "be" a word. Let the students "find their places" as they build each sentence. Ask the first and last student, "Why are you standing at the beginning (or end) of the sentence?" See if the first student can tell you that the capital letter at the beginning of his or her word helped determine where he or she would stand. Likewise, see if the last student can tell you that the period at the end of his or her word showed him or her where to stand. After each sentence is "built" by the children standing in the right order with their words in front of them, read the words aloud so the rest of the class can check to see if the sentence is correct.

Making a Class Book

After several sentences have been built, it is time for each child to cut apart the words in his or her own sentence and put the words back in the right order. Check to see that each word is in the correct place before allowing the children to paste the words down on their paper. Some students may still need some help with this, but others find it a simple task. Finally, have the students illustrate their sentences. When checking the sentences, you can also ask, "What are you going to draw?" Each child should be able to tell you that they are going to draw a mother doing something— that something is what they said as you wrote the predictable chart.

After the children have finished illustrating their sentences, help them to put the pages of the class book "in order." Use the predictable chart to help the children find their places. Add front and back covers to the book using colored construction paper, and write the title on the front in thick black magic marker. Now you have another class book to add to your collection. At the very end of the year, give one (or two) of the class-made books to each child as a souvenir of his or her time in kindergarten.

ENVIRONMENTAL PRINT-Restaurants

May and June are other months to focus on environmental print, so that children will walk or ride down the street and look for words they know and letters they can name over their summer vacation. Children need to "practice" at home some of the things they do in school, and one way to make sure they can do this is to use environmental print. You practiced letter names with cereal boxes last month. This month, focus on fast food restaurants. It is hard to drive in any city or town without seeing these restaurant signs. The bags and wrappers around the food that the students and their parents bring home advertise the restaurant's name and products it sells.

Talk about the different restaurants the students visit and see how many they can list. Bring in bags or food wrappers with these restaurant logos (names) on them. Most kindergarten children can "read" the logos of their favorite restaurants. Graph their favorites and see which restaurants are the most popular for the children in your classroom. Talk about these popular restaurants, discussing a different one each day.

For example, if Burger King® is the favorite restaurant, start with it. Hold up a Burger King® bag, and have the children look at it. Talk about the colors and the pictures (if any) on the bag. What does the Burger King® logo have to do with its name? Have the children count the letters in BURGER KING with you ("1-2-3-4-5-6-Space-7-8-9-10"). "There are 10 letters in BURGER KING." Then have the children say the letter names with you ("B-U-R-G-E-R -Space -K-I-N-G").

Next, pass out laminated cards with letter names on them. The letters should be identical to the letters on the bag or logo. Ask, "Who has the B? U? R? G? E? R? Space? K? I? N? G?" Have the children come to the front of the class and stand in the right order. As you point to each child holding a laminated letter card, have the student say his or her letter name. Then, collect the letters and ask the children to return to their seats.

Put the laminated letters in the pocket chart, then hold up the bag again. Ask the students "What do you notice about the words BURGER KING?" You may hear responses such as

"All the letters are capital."

"The bag is white."

"It begins with a *B* like *Bobby* or *Barbara*."

"BURGER KING is two words."

"You can hear the *k* sound at the beginning of KING."

"There are two *r*'s in BURGER KING."

After discussing the words BURGER KING, the logo, and the letters in the two words, let the children look at the laminated letters in the pocket chart and write the words BURGER KING on pieces of drawing paper with their black crayons or black markers. Then, have the children draw a picture of the restaurant, the logo, or the foods served at the restaurant.

Once you have done this activity with several restaurant names, you know that children will have another place to practice letter names. Young children enjoy showing what they have learned in school, and environmental print gives them that opportunity each day even if they do not come from homes with books and magazines.

Burger King Corporation is the exclusive license of the registered Burger King and Bun Halves Logo trademarks.

DEVELOPING PHONEMIC AWARENESS— Rhyming Books

Continue to read books that have some rhyming words. Let your students listen for the words and point them out when you reread the book. *Hop on Pop* by Dr. Seuss (previously cited) claims that it is "The Simplest Seuss for the Youngest Use." The book is filled with pages of rhyming words and funny pictures. Many children have read this book at home for years and will tell you, "That's a good book!" when you show it to them. On one page, the book shows a mouse on a house and on the next page, a house on a mouse. It has pages with words like *sad*, *dad*, *bad*, and *had*.

> "Dad is sad.
> He is very, very sad.
> He had a bad day.
> What a day Dad had."

Rounding Up the Rhymes

The first reading of this book is just to enjoy the book. The second time you read it, ask your students to listen for rhyming words as you read. Talk about the words that rhyme on each page. Let your students hear these words:

up	all	all	day	red
pup	tall	ball	play	bed
cup	small	wall		Ned
		fall		Ed

Write the words on the chalkboard or a chart. "What do you notice about these words?" Can students find the same spelling patterns, called "rimes," after the beginning sounds, called "onsets"? Can they add rhyming words to this list—*may*, *pay*, *say*, etc.?

Making Words

You can choose a rhyming pattern and "make words." Choose three children to be *a* and *l* and the other *l* and wear letter card necklaces or letter vests with these letters on the fronts. Have these children stand in front of the class. They spell *all* when they stand together. One by one, they are joined by the letters *b*, *c*, *h*, *w*, *f*, *m*, and then two-letter combinations like *sm* and *st*. Help the children to read each new word and to see the spelling pattern standing by itself when the beginning letter(s) leave.

Clapping Syllables

Another activity that helps children listen to words and separate them into the beats they hear is "clapping syllables." You can do this activity with summer words. Write *swim*, *pool*, *ocean*, *mountains*, *baseball*, *playing*, *book*, *bike*, and *sun* (or any other words you choose) on index cards to put in your pocket chart, or write the words on the chalkboard. Tell the children you are going to say these summer words and they should listen for the beats they hear. Ask the children to clap to show how many beats each word has. Say each word, one at a time. Help the children decide that *swim* is a one-clap word and that *ocean* takes two claps and is a two-beat word. Once you have said all ten words, do this again, pointing to the words as you clap the beats. Explain to the children that if a word has more claps or beats, it probably takes more letters to write. How many claps are in *vacation*? (Three)

Children who have been exposed to rhyming words, can hear rhymes, can see the spelling patterns in rhymes, and can add to a list of rhyming words with real or nonsense words, have developed the phonemic awareness that is so essential to learning to read.

WRITING BY CHILDREN—Young Authors' Conference or "Going Public"

It is now time to share what your students can and do write at school each day with their families. It is time for the "Young Author's Conference." If you have been saving the students' writing in a journal, folder, or on a disc, you already have the stories—now the children only have to decide which ones to publish. **Do not edit the children's stories; if you do, many children cannot read them.** Typing the stories makes it easier for everyone to read, but print them just as they are.

You have modeled stories and "think alouds" each day as you wrote on chart paper or the chalkboard. Continue to do this with stories about mothers, fathers, summer, picnics, field trips, end-of-the-year events, and things the students learned in kindergarten. As children finish "publishing" their book, they need to return to the writing process and write some more.

My Cat

I play with my cat.

I fed my cat.

My cat jops on the wendo.

My cat jops on my bad.

My cat wach me brsh my teth.

My cat is spashl to me.

Lensi

The Earth

It is so fun piceg up trash.

I want the earth to be clen.

I no that sumwun will halpe me.

If we have trash all over the earth we will not have H-2-O.

So thats wiy we net to clen up the earth.

Tac car of the earth so anomos can breth.

I glad sombuttle is halpeg me.

I net to clean up the earth.

The earth is still pertey.

Im a pes of the earth.

Adam

Show the children how you "make a book." First, take four or five pieces of plain paper and cut the pages in half. Then, use construction paper or index card stock paper and cut it in half, for the front and back covers. Staple or bind the pages and covers together to make a blank book. Usually, you can find a few mothers who will be glad to do this for the class and make 5-30 books at one time. Take a story that a child has written and that you have typed for easier reading. Print each sentence on a different line. If the story is less than five sentences, help the student to come up with more sentences.

Cut out the title of the story and paste it on the title page. Next, cut each sentence apart and paste it on a separate page. You can put a dedication page (at the beginning) in the book and an "About the Author" page (at the end) if you want. The children will then illustrate their pages. When the book has each sentence pasted on a page, and the children have illustrated each page, let the students practice reading their books to you and perhaps to other students who visit from some upper grade classes. This will give the students practice before the big day arrives when they read to their parents.

Some kindergarten teachers have punch and cookies for a "Young Author's Tea," usually held right before Mother's Day as a present to mothers of the children in the class. Sometimes, mothers and fathers are amazed to see so many five- and six-year-old children writing and reading!

CENTERS

Reading Center

Each center has a task for the students. The children get to practice reading and writing for real reasons as they read the signs in the centers and perform these tasks. Each week, the teacher finds tasks to enhance the themes. Planting and flowers are one theme this month; Mother's Day is another. The centers are tied closely to the themes and signs in the Centers. Books on summer (maybe travel folders and brochures) and favorite books read during kindergarten, along with lots of beginning readers, are found in the Reading Center.

Writing Center

The May Pictionary chart or bulletin board has words children want to write about at this time of year. You might want to put some materials in the Writing Center so that children can make journals to take home for summer writing. The computer is still popular with the children when they go to the Writing Center. You will notice that some children write longer stories when they have the help of a computer.

Restaurants (Center)

Since most kindergartners are familiar with restaurants, in May we can add a restaurant to our centers and show how real people read and write as they work. Into this center, we put menus or signs on the wall, order pads, tables, chairs, placemats, plates, utensils, food, credit cards, money, checks, and a cash register. Someone could be the cook reading orders and preparing the food (or pretending to cook). Someone could be the waiter or waitress writing the order (or pretending to write). You need lots of customers who read the menu, place their orders, and pay for their food.

ASSESSING PROGRESS

In order to determine how various children are developing in their reading, writing, and word knowledge, teachers need to be keen observers of children. The most practical diagnostic tool for this purpose is Marie Clay's *An Observation Survey of Early Literacy Achievement* (Heinemann Books, 1993). This survey, first developed as a screening device for Reading Recovery, has been adapted for classroom use. This survey is a valid and authentic measure of children's emergent literacy behaviors. This survey may become a part of kindergarten assessment.

Many teachers have come up with their own ways of observing children's early reading and writing progress. Here are some behaviors to observe as you assess student development, as listed in *Phonics They Use: Words for Reading and Writing* by P. Cunningham (HarperCollins, 1995):

Students read (or "pretend read") favorite books, poems, songs, and chants.

Students write in whatever way they can, and they can read what they wrote even if no one else can.

Students track print—they point to the words using left-right/top-bottom conventions.

Students know critical jargon—they can point to just one word, the first word in the sentence, just one letter, the first letter in the word, the longest word, etc.

Students recognize and can write some concrete words—their names and names of other children, days of the week, and favorite words from books, poems, and chants.

Students demonstrate phonemic awareness, orally manipulating words by taking off letters and changing the first letters to make words rhyme.

Students recognize words that rhyme and can make up rhymes.

Students can name many letters and can tell you words that begin with common initial sounds.

Students are learning more about the world they live in and are able to talk about what they know.

Students can listen to stories and informational books and retell the most important information. They see themselves as readers and writers and new members of the "literacy club."

Many children have hundreds of hours of literacy interactions at home during which they develop understandings critical to their success in beginning reading. **Our school programs must be structured to try to provide those experiences and interactions (that some children have already had) for all children.** This will not be an easy task. Schools do not have the luxury of providing these learning experiences one-child-at-a-time, but teachers can offer literacy learning in ways that simulate these home experiences as closely as possible.

CRITICAL UNDERSTANDINGS THAT ARE THE BUILDING BLOCKS TO SUCCESS

The multilevel reading and writing activities presented in this book are the building blocks to success for ALL kindergarten children. When understood and applied in the classroom, these critical understandings will be observed in young learners:

1) Children learn that reading provides both enjoyment and information, and they develop the desire to learn to read and write.

2) Students also learn many new concepts and add words and meanings to their speaking vocabulary.

3) Children learn print concepts, including how to read words from left to right, to read a page from top to bottom, etc.

4) Children develop phonemic awareness, including the concept of rhyme.

5) Students learn to read and write some interesting-to-them-words, like *Pizza Hut* and *cat*.

6) Students learn some letter names and sounds usually connected to the interesting words they have learned.

In developmentally appropriate kindergartens, teachers provide a variety of experiences so that all children develop these critical understandings which are the building blocks to success!

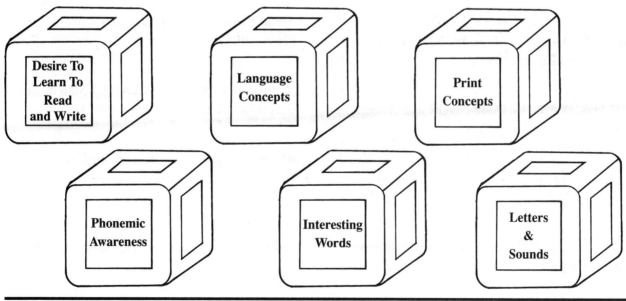

A is for Africa by Ifeoma Onyefulu (Cobblehill Books, 1993).

A, My Name is Alice by Jane Bayer (Dial Books, 1984).

A You're Adorable by Buddy Kaye et al. (Candlewick Press, 1994).

ABC and You by Eugenie Fernandes (Houghton Mifflin, 1996).

ABC Rhymes illustrated by R. W. Alley (D. C. Heath, 1991).

Accidental Zucchini: An Unexpected Alphabet by Max Grover (Harcourt Brace, 1993).

Alexander and the Terrible, Horrible, No Good, Very Bad Day by Judith Viorst (Aladdin Books, 1972).

Alexander, Who's Not (Do You Hear Me? I Mean It!) Going To Move by Judith Viorst (Atheneum Books, 1995).

All Aboard ABC by Doug Magee and Robert Newman (Philomel, 1993).

All about Seeds by Susan Kuchalla (Troll Assoc., 1982).

Alphabet City by Stephen T. Johnson (Viking Press, 1995).

Alphabet Tale, The by Jan Garten (Random House, 1964).

Alphabetics by Suse MacDonald (Bradbury Press, 1986).

Animal ABCs by Susan Hood (Troll Assoc., 1995).

Animal Mothers by Atsushi Komori (Putnam & Grossett, 1983).

Annie Bananie by Leah Komaiko (Scholastic, Inc., 1987).

Ape in a Cape: An Alphabet of Odd Animals by Fritz Eichenberg (Harcourt Brace, 1952).

Bears in Pairs by Niki Yektai (MacMillan, 1987).

Beginning To Read: Thinking and Learning About Print by Marilyn Jager Adams (MIT Press, 1994).

Berenstain Bears Go to Camp by Stan & Jan Berenstain (Random House, 1982).

Blueberries for Sal by Robert McCloskey (Viking Press, 1976).

Bright Eyes, Brown Skin by Cheryl Hudson and Bernette G. Ford (Just Us Books, 1990).

Brown Bear, Brown Bear, What Do You See? by Bill Martin, Jr. (Holt, Rinehart, and Winston, 1967).

Bug in a Jug and Other Funny Rhymes, A by Gloria Patrick (D. C. Heath, 1993).

Busy Year, A by Leo Lionni (Scholastic, Inc., 1992).

Buttons, Buttons by Rozanne Lanczak Williams (Creative Teaching Press, 1994).

By The Sea: An Alphabet Book by Anne Blades (Kids Can Press, 1985).

Carrot Seed, The by Ruth Krauss (HarperCollins, 1945).

Cat in the Hat by Dr. Seuss (Random House, 1957).

Chair For My Mother, A by Vera B. Williams (Wm. Morrow, 1984).

Chicken Soup with Rice by Maurice Sendak (Harper & Row, 1962).

Child's Year, A by Joan Walsh Anglund (Little Golden Books, 1992).

Christmas Time by Gail Gibbons (Holiday House, 1982).

City Mouse-Country Mouse (Aesop) pictures by John Wallner (Scholastic, Inc., 1989).

Color Dance by Ann Jonas (Greenwillow Books, 1989).

Corduroy's Christmas by B. G. Hennessy (Viking Press, 1992).

Country Fair by Gail Gibbons (Little, 1994).

Curious George by H.A. Ray (Houghton Mifflin, 1973).

Dibble and Dabble by Dave and Julie Saunders (Scott Foresman, 1996).

Dinosaurs Divorce: A Guide for Changing Families by Laurene and Marc Brown (Little, 1986).

Dr. Seuss's ABC by Theodore Seuss Geisel (Random House, 1963).

Each Peach Pear Plum by Janet and Allan Ahlberg (Viking Press, 1978).

Ear Book, The by Dr. Seuss (Random House, 1968).

Eating the Alphabet: Fruits and Vegetables from A to Z by Lois Ehlert (Harcourt Brace, 1989).

Eeny, Meeny, Miney Mouse by Gwen Pascoe and S. Williams (Houghton Mifflin, 1996).

"Emergent Literacy" by Elizabeth Sulzby and William Teale (*Handbook of Reading Research*, Vol. II, 1991).

Enormous Watermelon, The retold by Brenda Parkes and Judith Smith (Rigby, 1986).

Everett Anderson's Nine Month Long by Lucille Clifton (Henry Holt & Co., 1978).

First Snow by Emily Arnold McCully (Harper Trophy, 1985).

Five Little Monkeys Jumping on the Bed by Eileen Christelow (Clarion, 1989).

Foot Book, The by Dr. Seuss (Random House, 1968).

Franklin Goes to School by Paulette Bourgeois (Scholastic, Inc., 1995).

Frederick by Leo Lionni (Alfred A. Knopf, Inc., 1967).

From Acorn to Zoo and Everything in Between in Alphabetical Order by Satoshi Kitamura (Farrar, Straus, and Giroux, 1992).

Gingerbread Boy retold by Brenda Parkes and Judith Smith (Rigby, 1984).

Golden Bear by Ruth Young (Puffin Books, 1992).

Goldilocks and the Three Bears retold by David McPhail (D. C. Heath, 1989, 1991).

Goodnight Moon by Margaret Wise Brown (Scholastic, Inc., 1989).

Grandma's Helper by Lois Meyer (Scott Foresman, 1993).

Green Eggs and Ham by Dr. Seuss (Random House, 1960).

Green Queen, The by Nick Sharratt (Candlewick Press, 1992).

Growing Colors by Bruce McMillan (Lothrop, Lee, and Shepard Books, 1988).

Growing Vegetable Soup by Lois Ehlert (Harcourt Brace, 1987).

Gunnywolf, The retold by Antoinette Delaney (Scott Foresman, 1996).

Halloween by Miriam Nerlove (Albert Whitman, 1987).

Hanukkah by Gail Gibbons (Holiday House, 1986).

Harold and the Purple Crayon by Crockett Johnson (HarperCollins, 1955).

Hattie and the Fox by Mem Fox (Simon & Schuster, 1988).

Haunted House by Bill Martin, Jr. (Holt, Rinehart, and Winston, 1970).

Have You Seen My Cat? by Eric Carle (Putman & Grosset, 1988).

Hello, Snow! by Wendy Cheyette Lewison (Grosset & Dunlap, 1994).

Hop on Pop by Dr. Seuss (Random House, 1963).

Horrible Black Bug, The by Toni Jacquier (Rigby, 1988).

How Can I Help? by Christine Hood (Creative Teaching Press, 1996).

How Do Apples Grow? by Betsy Maestro (HarperCollins, 1993).

Hungry Caterpillar, The by Eric Carle (Scholastic, Inc., 1969, 1987).

I Am Special by Kimberly Jordano (Creative Teaching Press, 1996).

I Can't Get My Turtle To Move! by Elizabeth Lee O'Donnell (Houghton Mifflin, 1991).

I Know an Old Lady Who Swallowed a Fly illustrated by Slug Signorino (Scott Foresman, 1996).

I Like Rain by Claude Belanger (Shortland Publication, 1988).

I See Colors by Rozanne Lanczak Williams (Creative Teaching Press, 1995).

I Started School Today by Karen G. Frandsen (Children's Press, 1984).

I Went Walking by Sue Williams (Harcourt Brace, 1989).

In A People House by Dr. Seuss (Random House, 1989).

Is It Red? Is It Yellow? Is It Blue? by Tana Hoban (Mulberry Books, 1978).

It Begins with an A by Stephanie Calmenson (Hyperion, 1993).

It Looked Like Spilt Milk by Charles G. Shaw (Harper Trophy, 1988).

It's Pumpkin Time by Zoe Hall (Scholastic, Inc., 1994).

It's Spring! by Else H. Minarik (Greenwillow Books, 1989).

Jake Baked the Cake by B. G. Hennessy (Viking Press, 1990).

Johnny Appleseed by Steven Kellogg (Scholastic, Inc., 1988).

Just Like Daddy by Frank Asch (Aladdin Books, 1981).

K is for Kiss Goodnight: A Bedtime Alphabet by Jill Sardegan (Doubleday, 1994).

Katy and the Big Snow by Virginia Lee Burton (Scholastic, Inc., 1971).

Kindergarten Kids by Ellen Sensi (Scholastic, Inc., 1994).

Koala Lou by Mem Fox (Harcourt Brace, 1994).

Kwanzaa by Gail Gibbons (Holiday House, 1986).

"Literacy Knowledge in Practice: Contexts of Participation for Young Writers and Readers" by Susan Neuman and Kathleen Roskos *(Reading Research Quarterly,* Vol. 32, No. 1, 1997, pp. 10-32).

Little Engine That Could, The by Watty Piper (Putnam Publishing Group, 1984).

Little Red Hen by Janina Domanska (Houghton Mifflin, 1991).

Little Red Hen pictures by Lucinda McQueen (Scholastic, 1985).

Living Things by Judith Holloway (Modern Curriculum Press, 1990).

Look What I Can Do by Jose Aruego (Aladdin Books, 1971).

Mama, Do You Love Me? by Barbara M. Joosse (Chronicle Books, 1991).

Me Too! by Mercer Mayer (Houghton Mifflin, 1996).

Mike Mulligan and the Steam Shovel by Virginia Lee Burton (Houghton Mifflin, 1977).

Miss Nelson Is Missing! by Harry Allard (Scholastic, Inc., 1977).

Mitten, The retold by Jan Brett (G. P. Putnam's Sons, 1989).

Mitten, The by Krystyna Stasiak (Houghton Mifflin, 1991).

Molly's Pilgrim by Barbara Cohen (Bantam-Doubleday, 1995).

Monkeys in the Jungle by Angie Sage (Houghton Mifflin, 1991).

Monster Goes to School by Virginia Mueller (Albert Whitman, 1991).

"More More More," Said the Baby: Three Love Stories by Vera B. Williams (Scholastic, Inc., 1990).

Mr. Willowby's Christmas Tree by Robert Barry (McGraw Hill, 1963).

My Big Dictionary (Houghton Mifflin, 1994).

My Brown Bear Barney by Dorothy Butler (Greenwillow Books, 1989).

My Picture Dictionary edited by D. Snowball and R. Greene (Mondo, 1994).

Nana Upstairs, Nana Downstairs by Tomie De Paola (Puffin Books, 1978).

NBA Action from A to Z by James Preller (Scholastic, Inc., 1997).

Nine Days to Christmas by Marie Hall Ets (Puffin Books, 1991).

Observation Survey of Early Literacy Achievement, An by Marie Clay (Heinemann Books, 1997).

Old Man's Mitten: A Ukrainian Tale, The retold by Yevonne Pollock (Mondo, 1994).

On Market Street by Arnold Lobel (Greenwillow Books, 1981).

On the Go by Ann Morris (Scott Foresman, 1996).

One Fish, Two Fish, Red Fish, Blue Fish by Dr. Seuss (Random House, 1966).

100th Day of School, The by Angela Shelf Medevas (Scholastic, Inc., 1996).

One Tough Turkey by Steven Kroll (Holiday House, 1982).

Over in the Meadow by Sharon O'Neil (Harcourt, Brace, Jovanovich, 1989).

Owl Moon by Jane Yolen (Putnam & Grosset Group, 1987).

Ox-Cart Man by Donald Hall (Viking Press, 1979).

Phonics They Use: Words for Reading and Writing by P. Cunningham (HarperCollins, 1995).

Polar Bear, Polar Bear, What Do You Hear? by Bill Martin, Jr. (Henry Holt & Co., 1991).

Popcorn Book by Tomie De Paola (Scholastic, Inc., 1987).

Potluck by Anne Shelby (Scott Foresman, 1993).

Pretend You're A Cat by J. Marzollo (Dial Books, 1990).

Rain by Robert Kalan (Houghton Mifflin, 1996).

Real Mother Goose, The (Rand McNally & Co., 1916, 1944, 1976).

Relatives Came, The by Cynthia Rylant (Scholastic, Inc., 1985)

Rosie's Walk by Pat Hutchins (Aladdin Paperbacks, 1968).

Saturday Mornings by Joelie Hancock (Mondo, 1995).

School Bus by Donald Crews (Greenwillow Books, 1984).

School Days by B. G. Hennessy (Viking Press, 1990).

Seasons of Arnold's Apple Tree, The by Gail Gibbons (Harcourt Brace, 1988).

Sheep on a Ship by Nancy Shaw (Houghton Mifflin, 1989).

Sleepy ABC by Margaret Wise Brown (HarperCollins, 1994).

Snow on Snow on Snow by Cheryl Chapman (Dial Books, 1994).

Snowy Day, The by Ezra Jack Keats (Puffin Books, 1976).

Song and Dance Man, The by Karen Ackerman (Scholastic, Inc., 1988).

Spel...Is a Four Letter Word by J. Richard Gentry (Heinemann Books, 1989).

Story About Ping, The by Marjorie Flack and Kurt Weise (Viking Press, 1961).

Teaching Kids to Spell by J. Richard Gentry and Jean Wallace Gillet (Heinemann Books, 1992).

Thanksgiving Day by Gail Gibbons (Holiday House, 1984).

There's a Wocket in My Pocket by Dr. Seuss (Random House, 1974).

Things I Like by Anthony Browne (Houghton Mifflin, 1996).

This Is the Way We Go to School by Edith Baer (Scholastic, Inc., 1990).

Three Pigs, The retold by Brenda Parkes and Judith Smith (Rigby, 1985).

Timothy Goes To School by Rosemary Wells (Dial Books, 1981).

Today Is Thanksgiving! by P. K. Hallinan (Ideal's Children Books, 1993).

Too Many Tamales by Gary Soto (Scholastic, Inc., 1993).

Trip, The by Ezra Jack Keats (Greenwillow Books, 1978).

The Night Before Christmas by Clement C. Moore (American Greeting Co., 1976).

'Twas the Night Before Christmas in the Desert by Charlotte Van Bebber (Doe Eyes Publ., 1984).

Valentine's Day by Miriam Nerlove (Albert Whitman, 1992).

Vegetable Garden by Douglas Floring (Harcourt Brace, 1991).

Very Busy Spider, The by Eric Carle (Putnam & Grosset, 1988).

Watch Out For Chicken Feet in My Soup by Tomie De Paola (Puffin Books, 1974).

We Can Share at School by Rozanne Lanczak Williams (Creative Teaching Press, 1996).

We're Going on a Bear Hunt by Michael Rosen (HarperCollins, 1993).

What Is Christmas? by Lillie James (HarperCollins, 1994).

What Is Thanksgiving? by Harriet Ziefert (HarperCollins, 1992).

What Will the Weather Be Like Today? by Paul Rogers (Scholastic, Inc., 1989).

What's In My Pocket? by Rozanne Lanczak Williams (Creative Teaching Press, 1995.

Wheels on the Bus, The by Raffi (Crown, 1990).

When I Grow Up by Babs Bell Hajdusiewicz (Dominie Press, 1996).

When It Snows by JoAnne Nelson (Modern Curriculum Press, 1992).

When Will Santa Come? by Harriet Ziefert (HarperCollins, 1991).

Where Does the Butterfly Go When It Rains? by May Gorelick (Mondo, 1997).

Where Is Everybody? by Eve Merriman (Simon & Schuster, 1989; Big Book by Scott Foresman, 1996).

Where the Wild Things Are by Maurice Sendak (Scholastic, Inc., 1963).

White Is the Moon by Valerie Greeley (MacMillan, 1991).

White Rabbit's Color Book by Alan Baker (Kingfisher Books, 1994).

Who Said Red? by Mary Serfozo (Aladdin Books, 1992).

Who's in the Shed? by Brenda Parkes (Rigby, 1987).

Will You Be My Friend? by Eric Carle (Houghton Mifflin, 1991).

Winter: Discovering the Season by Louis Sentry (Troll Associates, 1983).

Wonder of Plants and Flowers, The by Laura Davon (Troll Assoc., 1990).

"You Can Analyze Developmental Spelling—And Here's How To Do It!" by J. Richard Gentry (*Early Years K-8,* May 1985).

Zoo-looking by Mem Fox (Mondo, 1995).